The Buddhist Way of Action

'We are all in one way or another in action twenty-four hours a day.' 'All things are in a state of flux, of perpetually becoming different.' 'All events and conditions arise by reason of previous events and conditions.'

With thoughts such as these in mind Christmas Humphreys, one of the most widely read proponents of Buddhism today and author of such popular books as *Buddhism, The Buddhist Way of Life*, and *Zen Buddhism*, set out to apply a philosophy based on Buddhist principles to the practical considerations of every-day life. In this richly varied book – originally entitled *The Way of Action* and now available as a paperback for the first time – he ranges over subjects such as love, friendship and compassion, duty and responsibility, right and wrong, good and evil, to the more abstract concepts such as action and inaction, mind-development and the form of existential thinking which is the Western approach to Zen. Written in a delightfully entertaining and lively style, it provides stimulating and thought-provoking reading for all those who question the possibility of leading a Buddhist way of life in the twentieth century.

'... lucid, practical, gentle, understanding and extremely persuasive.'

Anvil

'A book with a lively sincerity that entitles it to attention and respect.'

Philip Mairet, Time and Tide

MANDALA BOOKS

MANDALA BOOKS

Other Mandala Books include

I CHING: The Chinese Book of Change, a translation by John Blofeld
THE LIFE OF THE BUDDHA by H. Saddhatissa
LIGHT ON YOGA by B. K. S. Iyengar
MAN AND NATURE by S. H. Nasr
YOGA AND HEALTH by S. Yesudian and E. Haich
ZEN BUDDHISM by Christmas Humphreys
UNDERSTANDING ISLAM by Frithjof Schuon
RAMANA MAHARSHI by T. M. P. Mahadevan
MANTRAS by John Blofeld
HARA by Karlfried Dürckheim
SAMADHI by Mouni Sadhu
TAO TÊ CHING translated by Ch'u Ta-Kao
YOGA FOR HEALTH AND VITALITY by M. J. Kirschner
THE ART OF MEDITATION by Joel Goldsmith
THE WAY AND ITS POWER by Arthur Waley
COMPASSION YOGA by John Blofeld
CONCENTRATION by Mouni Sadhu
CREATIVE MEDITATION AND MULTI-DIMENSIONAL CONSCIOUSNESS by
    Lama Anagarika Govinda
ART AND THE OCCULT by Paul Waldo-Schwartz
THE ART OF SENSUAL MASSAGE by Gordon Inkeles and Murray Todris
DO-IT-YOURSELF SHIATSU by Wataru Ohashi

Other books by Christmas Humphreys include

BUDDHIST POEMS: A SELECTION 1920–1970
THE BUDDHIST WAY OF LIFE
A WESTERN APPROACH TO ZEN
EXPLORING BUDDHISM

The Buddhist Way of Action

A Working Philosophy for Daily Life

CHRISTMAS HUMPHREYS

A MANDALA BOOK
published by Unwin Paperbacks

Mandala Edition 1977
First published as 'The Way of Action' in 1960

ISBN 0 04 294100 8

Unwin Paperbacks
George Allen & Unwin (Publishers) Ltd
Ruskin House, Museum Street
London WC1A 1LU

Printed in Great Britain by
Butler & Tanner Ltd
Frome and London

Dedicated to Members of
The Buddhist Society

Preface

THIS book is a record of my own experience. As such it is deeply coloured with Buddhist thought, but it is not a Buddhist book, nor need it be added to any Buddhist library. It concerns the analysis of action, in the sense of right acting rather than right action, and the emphasis is therefore on the how and why of action rather than the what.

I have quoted liberally, partly to show that my own views, often seeming strange, have most respectable support, and partly because I like a well-turned phrase, and when another has said what I want to say far better than I could say it I let him say it again. Where I have not given full references it is because I found the quotation in a book in which the reference was not given. All references to the works of Dr Suzuki are to first editions, of which I am the proud possessor of a complete set, but those in possession of later reprints will easily find the equivalent passage.

I apologize for any confusion between Wei Lang and Hui-neng. The first translation of the famous Platform Sutra of the 6th Patriarch of Zen Buddhism was in a dialect which translated his name Wei Lang. Hence the book was called the *Sutra of Wei Lang*. Now we know better, and use the transliteration of Hui-neng. I have therefore called the book by its published title and the man Hui-neng.

I have used no diacritical marks for oriental terms in the text, partly because I deem it necessary that most of these terms, being untranslateable, should slowly be adopted into the English tongue, as others before them, such as Yoga and Nirvana. But certain marks have been added in the Glossary to help the reader to pronounce them properly.

The illustrations have been described by a friend as 'charmingly irrelevant'. Yet all are connected, at least in my mind, with the argument, as the captions show, and they are nice pictures.

I am grateful to Miss Amy Bedwell for long hours of fair-copying the revolting typing in which I have written books, without improvement, for thirty years; to the Ven. Sangharakshita, the Editor of the Maha Bodhi Journal of Calcutta, for permission to reprint two chapters, and for the same courtesy to Mrs Muriel Robins, Editor and almost re-creator of the Middle Way, the Journal of the Buddhist Society of 58 Eccleston Square, S.W.1

CHRISTMAS HUMPHREYS

London,
February, 1959.

THE purpose of this work may be set out in a few propositions and the conclusions to be drawn from them.

We are all, in one way or another, positively or negatively, in action twenty four hours a day. Even if we hold that right being is a superior condition to right acting we have a great deal to do before we learn to be.

All things are in a state of flux, of perpetually becoming different. In this process of change we have a choice of action only limited by the present results of our past choosing.

All events and conditions rise by reason of previous events and conditions. In common parlance, we are causing now effects that we shall experience later.

We should not be respectively writing and reading this book if we had not in our flow through life already adopted some ideal condition to achieve or become, or were striving to formulate such a condition.

It follows that the more right our acting now the quicker we shall achieve that ideal by the operation of the law of cause/effect.

There can be no more important task for us, therefore, now, than to find out what is right acting, and to attempt to make every one of our actions 'right'.

This, the technique of right acting, is to be distinguished from the far wider field of the right thing to do. The Sermon on the Mount and the Dhammapada, for example, both contain a magnificent list of right things to do, but here we are primarily concerned with right doing, with the how of action rather than the what. Perhaps in the end we shall find that they are the same.

In brief, as we are doing something all the time let us learn to do it rightly.

From these principles I have derived

THE WAY OF ACTION

It may be formulated thus:

An entire and sufficient working philosophy of life may be

11

devised about the right doing of the act in hand, whatever it may be.

If this act is rightly done, the actor on his way through life will find a diminishing need of assistance from philosophic doctrine, religious practice or a Saviour of any kind. In harmony with the rhythm of life, he will be able safely to ignore such man-made distinctions as being and doing, right action and wrong action, and by concentrating on the utterly right performance of the next thing to be done, move happily towards his own and the world's enlightenment.

If it be true, and I hold it to be true, that 'the immediate work, whatever it may be, has the abstract claim of duty, and its relative importance or non-importance is not to be considered at all', then the next thing to be done, and rightly done, is sufficient agenda for any man for twenty four hours a day. But it must be rightly done, and much is wound up in the syllable right. Let us try to unravel it.

Contents

Illustrations

Introduction

As explained in the Prologue, even though Being is superior to Acting we all have a great deal to do before we learn once more to 'be'. We shall not attain to Being by stating it as an admirable ideal. At present we are far from that condition and must seek a way from what we are to what we would be. How? In the words of a Chinese classic, 'the secret of the magic of life consists in using action to achieve non-action'. From action to Non-action, that is the path, and we are all treading it, however it is described on the map we choose for the journey. In terms of Indian Yoga the way is described as threefold; Jnana Yoga, the way of the intellect, that of the philosopher; Bhakti Yoga, the way of devotion to the loved ideal, that of the mystic and the religious devotee, and Karma Yoga, the way of action in the world of men as described in the Bhagavad Gita. All three are 'right', for all are facets of one trinity, but it would seem that we in the West are predominantly Karma Yogins. We seek to know, to understand, to become, by doing, and in every walk of life we respect efficiency in action. It is not without interest that Yoga itself is generally described as 'skill in action', and action is discernable in the least moment of our lives. Indeed, we cannot conceive of Being without action, or if we form the concept it is no more than such, and does not eliminate the need for right action to become what we conceive. But this is itself a matter of training, of long and rigorous training. In summarizing the benefits of Yoga practice, Patanjali says, 'The mind that has been so trained that the ordinary modifications of its action are not present, but only those which occur on the conscious taking up of an object for contemplation, is changed into the likeness of that which is pondered upon, and enters into the full comprehension of the being thereof.'[1]

But before the mind is ready even to begin to re-become that Essence of Mind which is its nature there is much to be done. Hence Part One of this book, a brief analysis of some of the ingredients of action. There will then be time enough to go Into Action, in Part Two, and to end with a brief description of

[1] Number 41. Trans. W. Q. Judge.

how a group of Western students find that these ideas and practices may be applied to daily life, and with what result.

First, we must view the Field of Action, no less than the universe, that 'boundless plane which is periodically the playground of numberless universes incessantly manifesting and disappearing as a regular tidal ebb of flux and reflux'.[1] We must toy for a while with the concepts of metaphysics, of the Absolute and the relative and the relationship, or none, between them, of God and his creations or, as Eckhart puts it better than the modern Christians, of the Godhead which is anterior to God. Only by a working knowledge of the primeval One and its derivatives of Two and Three can we understand the basic duality of our lives, and dimly conceive the Non-duality behind the vast diversity. Only from such a sense of oneness will arise compassion, the perpetual awareness that life is one though in a million forms, or large or small, and that the suffering and joy of each is that of all. In such a field, most of it beyond our senses and beyond the range of all but the most tenuous concept, walks man, an animal not yet wholly adapted to his environment yet in his mind at best a god. Which reigns, the god or beast, is for each to decide in their joint territory; in most of us it is a divided and alternate throne. But we must look at man more closely before we see how and when, and why, he acts.

Of the analysis of self there is no end, nor is any one description of the parts ever likely to satisfy mankind. St Paul's trinity of body, soul and spirit stands up well through the centuries as empirically satisfactory, but modern analyses must take into account the re-discovery of the Unconscious as a factor in psychology as distinct from philosophy. But the divers 'selves', the self, the Self and SELF, and a dozen other descriptions, are matters of doctrine rather than components of action, and the purpose of the brief analysis in Chapter Two is rather to draw attention to the complexity of that which acts than to describe its parts seriatim.

Meanwhile, whoever the actor is he spends the greater part of his time in acting wrongly, by any criterion. The catalogue of wrong actions could well fill a book, but the reader's mind is

[1] From the Proem to *The Secret Doctrine* by H. P. Blavatsky.

being applied in the first place to right acting, and consequent right action, and it is well to appreciate the basic wrongness of our average present life. Too many humans have no aim or purpose of any kind; still less by right means are they learning to be. Flabbiness of purpose, vagueness of means, inefficiency of action, these and wasted effort on all planes are ripe causes of unhappiness, and happiness, however vaguely conceived, is the goal of most of mankind. To aim high and fall is one thing; to aim so low as personal happiness and to fail for want of precision of purpose and means, here is failure indeed. If it is untrue that 'there is no health in us', it is true that until we face the futility of nine tenths of our existence we are not likely to move towards right acting, much less to direct acting, and thence to Non-action, wherein alone lies joy beyond all happiness.

Here, then, is the infinitely tiny part in the vast field of the Whole. The relation of one to the other is basic in the concept of right acting. The subjective and objective points of view, desire and non-desiring, the concentric circles of possessions about the mind, from the physical body to the neighbourhood wherein one lives, and from the habitual reaction to others' thoughts to one's own projected concept of the far ideal, all these are important to the conscious actor of right acts, and both are changing in relation to each other constantly. We lightly speak of a youth as maladjusted, to his environment, his family, his job, but are any of us fully adjusted, consciously, to nature and humanity, the past and the future, our enemies and friends, our various possessions? Few psychiatrists would answer yes in respect of any man. And in the mutual change between man and circumstance is more than social adjustment; there is a full philosophy of life.

The secret of right relationship is, of course, a Middle Way, and on this the Buddha based his message to mankind. From the simple analysis of the Theravada scriptures, of a middle way between the extremes of asceticism and self-indulgence, to the exquisitely subtle 'middleness' of the later schools of the Mahayana in which both of the opposites disappear, here is a great adventure in philosophy, morality and metaphysics, leading back to the source of the universe itself. But it is a way and not a theory, a path for all of us who seek right acting, and although in one sense it pertains to doctrine, in another it is the very heart of what we are now describing.

But this consideration has brought up further problems in relationship which are worth description on their own. Hence a chapter on Rights and Duties and Responsibilities, and a brief description of a theory dear to me, that we Pay As We Go. Then follow the main considerations of our thesis, Action and Inaction, Action and Reaction, and Action and Interaction. The first deals with the objection that not to act is wiser than most action. The distinction is false, for inaction is itself a form of action and very often a bad one. Action and passivity, these are but another of the Pairs of Opposites, which cannot be apprehended save from the viewpoint of a 'higher third', the apex of a triangle which alone gives each its use and meaning. This is more easily seen in Action and Reaction, in which is discussed the most profound teaching in all Eastern philosophy. For the law of Karma seems to be the basic law of the manifestation of the universe, and every other law, of nature, science and man is included and subsumed in it. 'This being so, that becomes; from the arising of this that arises; this not becoming, that does not become; from the ceasing of this that ceases.' Is there any more to be said? As the centuries rolled by after the Buddha's passing a vast edifice of teaching was erected on the foundation of these few words. But this is the charter of right acting, not of belief, and even as the architect must use, and rightly use the law of gravity in all his building, so the man of action, and all are such, must use the law of Karma to become what he would be. But if it be true that the effects of the least action ripple out to the margins of the universe and thence return, it follows that the countless units of life are affecting each other every moment, for 'good' or 'ill', and not a sparrow falls but all the universe shall know it.

The chapter on Action and Interaction covers the relationship of wisdom and compassion, the latter being presented as the necessary expression of the former. If it be true, as I have written elsewhere, that 'all men serve self, but a man may be measured by the size of the self he serves', then we cannot ignore the Whole of which each self is part. Yet we cannot serve mankind, or even our neighbour, save by what we are, and it may be that the surest way to help others is so to develop one's own awareness of the Essence of Mind that its light is visible to all.

So much for the ingredients of Action. Has the time, then, come for going Into Action? Not for the moment, for first there is the bridge to face, and cross, between intention and its execution, between seeing the thing to be done, and arising to do it. The deadweight of inertia is heavy indeed, and if the ultimate goal is right Being, it is strange that we find it so intolerably difficult to begin to do what needs to be done before that goal is achieved. This chapter is, from the author's point of view, the beginning and the end of the book, though its place is rightly in the middle. The first half of the book leads up to it, and the second half assumes that the bridge is crossed. It might be said that he who sees the bridge and crosses it will find the way for himself. It may be so, but words can encourage the facing of facts, and the gap between right resolve and the first step of right action is a large fact indeed. In a sense it is the moment of 'conversion', that 'turning about at the seat of consciousness', as it is described in Mahayana philosophy, which results in the new man no longer facing the world of the senses but inwards, upwards, home.

Part Two, then, deals with Action itself, but always with priority of attention to the acting rather than the act. Chapter Eleven, which may be variously described as Ways to the One, or Methods, Schools and Devices, speaks for itself, and stresses the need of tolerance in considering the way that is chosen by another. 'Let each man prove his own work' is good advice, and the word prove meant to show forth as sound in workmanship. Verily, 'by their fruits ye shall know them', and the test of any method is that it works. If it works for another, why be rude about it, even though you are certain that it would not work for you? The time and energy exerted by those who, having found a good way for themselves, force it as a universal panacea down the throats of those who are equally content with their own way is a witness to the conceit of man and his ignorance of the vast variety of manifested things. But of the many ways available, one of the best known to the world is the Buddha's Eightfold Path to Enlightenment, and a description is therefore given of the Way which he trod from such as we now are to what he became. Even here, however, emphasis is given to right acting; we need but little counsel for right action, for it has been said that if all men applied the Sermon on the Mount we should need but little more.

The last three steps on the Path are concerned with mind-development, which is to the Eastern mind the principal if not the sole concern of any man. Some of the greatest Scriptures are concerned with nothing else, and in the world today the pressure of life is driving more and more intelligent men and women, in Tokyo and Rangoon, as in London and New York, back to the world of peace which lies within, the serenity which may be found in a mind which has dropped entanglements and is content to strive to be. But the steps of mind-development are clearly marked. First there must be the power of concentration on a given object, and the power to drop that object at will. Only then can the mind begin to meditate, 'with seed' or 'without seed', that is, with a subject or without. But the fruits of true meditation belong to a plane beyond that of thought, and this plane cannot be attained until the distinction between the intellect and the intuition is clearly and effectively known. Hence the chapter, From Intellect to Intuition, which attempts to introduce the student to a distinction not yet achieved, it would seem, by Western psychology. Yet only by the use of the intuition, the special faculty of enlightenment, can the goal of action, Direct Action, be attained, and in practice this is a distinction difficult to prove to the average Westerner. Once it is grasped he can begin to apply the advice of Bodhidharma, the founder of Zen. 'No dependence on words and scriptures; direct pointing to the soul of man.' Direct action alone, immediate, purposeless, will point to that Essence of Mind which, intrinsically pure, is the soul of man and of the universe. But what can one say of it? The answer is little, and still less of that which follows, Non-action itself, that which contains all action and inaction and all its correlates, but which is one with the Void which yet is full, with that Wisdom (Prajna) which is that of the Absolute.

Perhaps there should then be a chapter on Nirvana, the Buddhist 'Heaven'. But 'we can as well represent Enlightenment by means of explanation or analysis as we do personality by snapshots or anatomical operations'.[1] True, it is basic Buddhism that Nirvana and its opposite, Samsara, the round of rebirth, are one and the same, two aspects of one Reality, but this is itself a truth which lies on the plane of Enlightenment. It is equally true to say that Nirvana being what it is there is no such thing to be attained, but these are words, words as the symbols of ideas and concepts; the truth must for the while elude us until that day when, bursting through the illusion of the bonds which bind us, we know what we are, and live accordingly. Meanwhile, it is right to say that the most we can know of Nirvana is the Way to it, and it is therefore wisdom to tread that way. Let us walk on.

[1]Kaiten Nukariya, *The Religion of the Samurai*, p. 123.

PART I

The Ingredients of Action

Chapter 1

The Field of Action

Tao begets One; One begets two; two begets three; three begets all things.   TAO TÊ CHING

The One is none other than the All, the All none other than the One.
Take your stand on this, and the rest will follow of its own accord.   SHINJIN-NO-MEI

THE field of action is the manifested universe, nor does it very much matter for our purposes whence it came or why from the Unmanifest. The Buddha enjoined his Bhikkhus not to waste time on such enquiries, for the answers, even if obtained, would not 'conduce to the holy life, to enlightenment, to Nirvana'. But the West is more materialistic, though its materialism is largely cloaked under the guise of science, and some of the 'working principles' of this ultimate field of thought may help in the search for right acting. Certainly, the Mahayana schools of Buddhism quickly developed a range of magnificent abstract thought which, as the innermost veils about the light of Truth, transcend all other thinking. Their conclusions refuse to be crushed into the pigeon-holes beloved of Western thinkers, who carve the living Truth into the categories of philosophy and metaphysics, religion and mysticism, ontology, epistemology and psychology, forgetting or not knowing that these are facets of Mind-only, which can no more be carved into fragments than a man with a carving knife can cut up the sea. The East, with its more synthetic, intuitive and total approach to Reality, which it seeks in meditation rather than in the lecture hall, is as willing to descend from a traditional general principle to resultant particulars as western science is to argue from a number of particulars to a tentative generalization.

Stripped of their lovely clothes of poetry and symbolism, these basic truths of the universe as taught in the Mahayana may be stated in terms of Nothing, and One, Two, Three. The rest is commentary and explanation, to be found in diverse forms in the mythology of every nation, however primitive, and in the philosophy of the greatest, as in India, China and Tibet.

The Absolute and the One

First is the ABSOLUTE, the Parabrahman of Indian wisdom, the Uncreated and Unformed of the Buddhist scriptures, the God-head as distinct from the manifest God of the deeper Christian teaching which Eckhart understood so well. This, the 'unuttered God' is indeed, as Eckhart said, 'a nameless nothingness', in the Hindu phrasing, THAT in the approach to which all concept fails and falls to the ground. This 'Omnipresent, Eternal Boundless and Immutable Principle', as H. P. Blavatsky calls it, indeed 'transcends the power of human conception and could only be dwarfed by any human expression or similitude. It is beyond the range and reach of thought.' Let us call it the Absolute.

It has no relation with the relative world in which we live. This is a hard saying but surely obvious. All relationship reduces thereby the stature of the parties. The Absolute cannot be reduced, or it is not the Absolute. It can only be conceived in its first emanation, its mask in the field of the relative. We know this mask, this first becoming, as the One. This Oneness is for us the centre from which all radiates, the goal to which all returns, the criterion of all right action and the meaning of everything. It is not, however, the Absolute, and to Buddhist thinkers goes the honour of first making this clear to the simplest mind. 'If all is reduced to the One', said a Zen Master, 'to what is the One reduced?' For the One is the opposite to the Many, and only Something beyond the One can subsume the One and the Many.

In one sense the Absolute, which is Non-Duality as distinct from One, created duality when it assumed the mask of Oneness. We can more easily consider this, however, in terms of the two-ness which came from the One.

This One, as the manifest Absolute, itself remains unchanged, yet the very basis of Zen thought, and, it would seem, of the accumulated wisdom of the ages, is that this One is All. In these three words lies the heart of esoteric Buddhism. This is not pantheism; it is infinitely more. As Dr Suzuki puts it, 'the phrase "One in All" and "All in One" is to be understood as a complete statement of absolute fact, and not to be analysed into its component concepts. When an object is picked up everything else, One and All, comes along with it, not in the way of suggestion but all-inclusively, in the sense that the object is complete in itself.'[1] This is the basis of the Kegon philosophy of Jijimuge, of the 'uninterrupted interdiffusion of all particulars' with each other. Herein the doornob *is* the orange and the orange *is* the doornob, not relatively, comparatively or indirectly, as species of one genus, but absolutely, directly and precisely as declared. Here is no pantheism, wherein all things are one with God because God is everything but, as the same author wrote in *The Essence of Zen*, 'All is God and there is no God.' The difference in right action will be found tremendous; if so, our brief incursion into Buddhist thought will not have been made in vain.

Put otherwise, we have the great declaration that Samsara, the world as we know it, and Nirvana, the state of enlightened perfection, are indissolubly one. In the same way Tathata, the essential 'Suchness' of everything, which makes it what it is and not otherwise, and Sunyata, the absolute Void which yet is full, the nothingness of things, are one, viewed differently, and Tennyson was right when he pondered over the 'flower in the crannied wall'.

Much follows. Here one may point out a single consequence. If completeness is a perquisite of the One, and all our efforts attain but to comparative completeness, then the Greeks were right when saying that the half is often greater than the whole. The whole is the whole and arouses nothing within us; the part is infinite, and all creation moves in to complete it, to perfect it, to make it equal to the unattainable whole.

The One divides
Then the One divides. Why? Why did God create the Universe? That He might know Himself. The Absolute is absolutely

[1] *Zen Buddhism and its Influence on Japanese Culture*, pp. 27-8 and 14.

unconscious, and can have no awareness of itself. For this would mean three things, a knower, a known and knowledge. Therefore, that the One may know itself it must become two; it must create a mirror in which to see itself. Dante put it well: 'Not for His own greater good—to the Good no good can be added—but that His splendour might have power to say "I am".'[1] And the One is the great 'I am'. All parts are this or that; only the Total *is*.

But it matters not why the One became Many, why the Unmanifest, sleeping the long 'night of Brahma', once more unrolled itself on the field of 'absolute, abstract space' as 'absolute, abstract motion'. It did so, and that which was One became One-yet-Two. This non-existent moment, the moment of dawn when the night is not yet day yet is no longer night, is of enormous value to the seeker. We know it in meditation where it lies between knowing and that Not-knowing which alone is Prajna, the Wisdom of Non-Duality.

Then Two is born, and with it the myriad 'apparent distinctions' referred to in the *Tao Tê Ching*. Spirit and matter, life and form, the positive Yang and the female Yin, forth they come, the innumerable Pairs of Opposites on which the manifested universe is built, and in the polarity or tension between which all the processes of life take place. Once this rhythm is established, between in-breathing and out-breathing, night and day, effort and passivity, breaking down and building up, the field is prepared for that exercise of free-will which, limited only by the effects of its previous use, determines what action we take, with what purpose and with what effect. Above all, for our present purposes it is the field of concept, of 'thought-things', of those things which are forces powerful enough to sway nations, and binding enough to hold the unreal mind in thrall.

Then comes Three, for Duality in itself is not only unstable but an impossible concept to conceive. No mind can conceive two without a relation between them (for no-relation is itself a relation), and the relationship makes three. On this basic Trinity many religions are founded, for the One is a difficult concept, and three, poetically personalized as Father, Mother

[1] Paradiso xxix, 13. Trans. Warner Allen in *The Timeless Moment*, p. 161.

and Son, or Creator, Preserver and Destroyer, is easier for the mind to grasp and use. But the Three may be placed six ways, with a seventh central point of synthesis; thus Seven, and so to Ten, the Twelve of the Zodiac and much besides, and so to the Many which the Chinese call the 'ten thousand things'.

If this be a crude presentation of the ultimate structure of the universe, it is sufficient for our purpose here, and it has the merit that it 'works' in the reflected pattern of our daily lives. 'As above, so below', is an ancient maxim, and at the lowest point of the long descent from Spirit to Matter it is well to have some miniature of the cosmic pattern or plan in mind.

The relation of the Many to the One is of great importance. In most of the world's religions and philosophies there is a movement 'from the unreal to the real, from darkness to light, from death to immortality', to use the Hindu phrasing. This, in Buddhist eyes, is only half the story. For 'when all things are reduced to the One, to what is the One reduced?', a famous question we shall ask ourselves again and again. In Buddhist philosophy there is no such movement to a final goal, for it is but a swing between the Opposites, from hell to heaven, from matter to spirit, and on the pendulum of duality the swing-back will, in the illusion of time, return to the point whence it came.

The Buddhist teaching passes beyond the Opposites, and bravely restores not only the Two to One but the Two and the One to that which alone transcends them. This teaching of Jijimuge, as already described, announces the self-identity of all the Opposites, and the effect on daily life is enormous. If life is motion then all is change. Things *must* become different, we *must* grow old and die. The present situation, good, bad or indifferent as we care to label it, will not remain. Security is an illusion; there is wisdom alone, as Alan Watts has pointed out to us, in insecurity and its free acceptance.[1] We must learn to accept the 'incessant multiplication of the inexhaustible One and unification of the indefinitely Many. Such are the beginnings and endings of worlds and individual beings: expanded from a point without position or dimensions and a now without date or duration, accomplishing their destiny, and when their time

[1] Alan Watts: *The Wisdom of Insecurity.*

is up returning "home" to the Sea in which their life originated.'[1]

The Concept of God

In particular we must revise our concept of God. That God exists, as a thought-form of enormous power projected by the minds of men beyond the ambit of the psyche, is beyond question. From another point of view men have personalized and hypostasized some chosen aspect of the One and given it false existence as a separate entity. To the Buddhist 'God' has no greater meaning than this. He is not THAT which created the universe, for THAT, as already seen, is beyond all predicates, and has no relation whatsoever with the parts, or any of them, of the Whole. Of Gods, however, there are many, ranging from personifications of cosmic powers, and the Gods of divers religions and nations, through the ancient kingdoms of 'Angels, Thrones, Dominations and Powers' to the humblest tree-god of a savage tribe. Yet none is a Saviour in the objective sense that from such a Person or Power can come any divine, non-human force which is capable of affecting the destiny of the individual. 'Work out your own salvation, with diligence' were the Buddha's final words, and with the single exception of the Shin sect of Japanese Buddhism, no body of Buddhists would ignore that final advice.

For the man who seeks right action this is of practical value, for when the relation of the individual to the Whole is clarified and understood, his relations with his fellow men and all creation will be clarified accordingly. Compassion, for example, from a somewhat forced interest in the needs of others becomes as much a personal concern as the daily needs of the family as a whole. More important, however, is the effect of 'Self-identity of Opposites' on the search for enlightenment. We in the West are prone to seek salvation, or whatever we term the object of our search, in Heaven, a state to be attained after death. But if Heaven is here and now, in a wild flower as in a cathedral, the outgoing effort to attain may be withdrawn inward, the objective search made entirely subjective, the process of doing be reduced to the means of becoming what we already are. 'Look within thee,' says *The Voice of the Silence*, 'thou art

[1] Coomaraswamy: *Hinduism and Buddhism*, p. 9.

Buddha.' 'The Light is within thee', said the Egyptian Hiero-
phants of old, 'Let the Light shine.' This Light is not only in
Heaven, but is here and now, shining out of everything if we
had but eyes to see it. It shines through the cracks of what the
author of *Neti Neti*, L. C. Beckett, calls the Nothing Between,
and we are blind to it. As Francis Thompson wrote:

> Does the fish soar to find the ocean,
> The eagle plunge to find the air—
> That we ask of the stars in motion
> If they have rumour of thee there?
>
> Not where the wheeling systems darken,
> And our benumbed conceiving soars!—
> The drift of pinions, would we hearken,
> Beats at our own clay-shuttered doors.
>
> The angels keep their ancient places;—
> Turn but a stone and start a wing!
> 'Tis ye, 'tis your estrangéd faces,
> That miss the many splendoured thing. . . .

In this vast field of cosmic manifestation, from the 'nights of
Brahma' through 'the days of Brahma' and back into the long,
unmanifest night, man, then, is a part of the whole that is at one
and the same time relative and absolute. Yet whether we understand, however dimly, this vast aeonic process of the out-
breathing and in-breathing of the manifested universe is of
little moment. The Buddha did, for he said so. 'The arising of
the world, O Bhikkhus . . . the ceasing of the world, O Bhikkhus,
hath been fully understood by the Tathagata, as also the way
that leads to it.' For ourselves it is sufficient to accept as a
working hypothesis that it is so.

Now, Here and This

If it is, then time and space are relative concepts, and time is a
process which is integrated with the human mind. But the way
in which we divide it is, though convenient, fallacious when we
consider things as they are. We freely speak of the past and the
future but we have no experience of them. Speaking at any
moment, the past is a matter of memory, a concept or thought-
form of what is remembered as having happened to the then

condition of the ever-changing thing called self. In the same way we never know the future. It is but a thought-form built up of memory and much beside and projected into a non-existent period of time for our convenience, or, when we are consumed with anxiety, for our inconvenience. What, then, is the present? It does not exist. The swiftest thinking cannot catch the moment when the past is gone and the future not yet come. The present is a concept for a state of consciousness which, because its speed of change is enormous embraces a little of the past in memory, a little of the future in anticipation, and the non-existent moment of now. But Now is a different matter. The eternal Now is a fact of experience well known to the West since at least the days of Eckhart, who spoke of it frequently. In the Now all things are present and all events take place. Here is the 'one thought-moment' of Zen which comes from the 'Nothing Between', the moment of super-normal because super-conceptual awareness when we 'see' things as they are in their naked Tathata or 'suchness', in their nature as Sunya, empty (of abiding qualities or being), and as Nirvana, which is a quality of all things, of the dish-cloth as of the Buddha.

But all is not only Now but Here and This. It is a fascinating thought that we are always here. If we move across the room, or the world, we are still 'here' even though the here be different. The past and future forms of 'here' are now but memories or anticipations. Only the present here is here, and now. And 'this', this thing in hand is all we directly know. A this which is past is a memory, and that which is not yet come is not yet this. Our consciousness, then, is always concentrated on this which is here and now; all else is second-hand experience, a toying with concepts which begin to die as soon as formed. They have no part or lot in right action, in the motiveless performance, with the right means, of the task which is here and now and with this. The result of this possibly new point of view is quite consider-able. With only the moment and its duties in the field of aware-ness we can relax the tensions produced by smug satisfaction or regret, by desire for a moment not yet born or fear of it, and relax in Now. Concerned alone with now we are only con-cerned with causes and not with effects. If the cause be rightly created now we need not trouble about the correctness of the effect. We are standing on our own two feet, upright, un-shakeable; we are no longer leaning so far into the future to view the unborn effect that if the effect should turn out other-wise we should fall on our faces.

This fleeting vision of 'the destruction and renewal of aeons', as the Buddhist Scriptures have it, helps to create the right perspective from which to view the field of action on which the actor, man, struts for his tiny hour. Its implications are endless. If the absolute and the relative are indissolubly interdiffused there must be an Absolute Truth which we may not know in the relative, and a relative Truth which we handle day by day. This comforts us, for we know that in our search for right action we can only approximate nearer and nearer to the scarcely seen ideal.

There is no death

Much else follows. If all is One then all is law. We know some of the laws of the universe, but a cosmic scheme in which there is a blend of law and lawlessness is quite unthinkable. There is, then, cosmic law and a thousand laws within it. But if all is One then all is life, all is alive, and there is no death. There is a cycle that we see of birth and growth and decay and death, but the death is the dissolution of the form in which some part of life had gained its partial expression. The form dissolves when life moves on to another form; the life can never die. And how can there be two lives in this flower and in that, in this molecule and that, in you and me? Life, our vague term for the force or motion which is one of the two components of the Two, the other being space or form, is half the Absolute, if such nonsense be permitted; its other half is the forms of the Many, the manifold vestures of the life which is One. All lives are there-fore one life, and all things, being the same life in its divers forms, are truly brothers, not as a sentimental ideal but as a fact in nature, as the spinning earth or spring-time or a worm. Compassion, then, has roots in reason and not in sentiment. We are brothers; let us behave as brothers should. The impli-cations of this implication, so to speak, are also endless and we shall return to them later.

But the cycle of the birth and death of the universe has cycles within it. Always there seems a double process simultaneously, of spirit descending into matter and matter returning, as the Prodigal Son, whence it came. Always some things are going 'from bad to worse', as it seems to us, and some from good to better. In cycles large and small we move up and down, on the rising cycle of yet more life, on the falling arc to the death of the form which has had its day. This dual movement helps the acceptance of the theory of rebirth, for work and rest are another of the Pairs of Opposites, and after a life of causes there must be time for the due digestion of effects.

This rhythmic movement of a cosmic process is the basis for right timing. There is a time for all things, as many a scripture well describes, or, as an Arabic proverb has it, 'Thou canst not mount the camel that has gone nor the camel that has not yet come.' Patience is a virtue when it relates to right timing; a vice when it conceals inertia and the laziness that will not act at all. 'To act and act wisely when the time for action comes, to wait and wait patiently when it is time for repose, puts man in accord with the rising and falling tides of affairs so that, with nature and law at his back, and truth and beneficence as his beacon light, he may accomplish wonders.'[1]

From this it is easier to glimpse the cosmic harmony of nature and all therein. I have long delighted in the somewhat ponderous observations of the Emperor Marcus Aurelius to this effect. 'Constantly picture the universe as a living organism, controlling a single substance and a single soul, and note how all things react upon a single world-sense, all act by a single impulse, and all co-operate towards all that comes to pass; and mark the contexture and concatenation of the web.'

The field of action, then, is vast indeed, and in it, lost in terms of size but large perhaps in spiritual significance, walks man. Let us look at him, this actor in the field of action.

---

[1] From an article signed 'J.D.B.' in *The Path*, ed. by William Q. Judge, in July 1889.

Chapter 2

The Actor

*What we call the self is the most complex thing
in existence.*   NOEL TEMPLE

THE Absolute is the invisible and yet omnipresent factor in
every thing which emanated from it; it is the 'suchness' or 'isness'
of it which makes it what it is. Yet no thing, nor any collection
of things, can claim to be the Absolute.

But 'As above, so below', and man is a microcosm of the
macrocosm, the universe in miniature, as even the atom is now
found by scientists to be. In him too is 'the Unborn, Unbecome,
Uncreated, Incomposite', as it is called in the Buddhist Scriptures, but it is not his alone, nor can any man call this Spirit or
Atman or the God-within his personal property. In brief, there
is nowhere in man an 'immortal soul', unchanging and unique,
which is utterly his alone, and the flat denial of such an entity
forms the Buddhist doctrine of Anatta. This is the declaration of
the interdependence of all phenomena, for all things, vast or
infinitesimal in size, are alike the product of preceding groups
of phenomena, the fleeting forms of one life, the myriad manifestations of the Absolute which, while clothed for a while in
the garments of the universe yet, beyond time and space,
uniquely unaffected, IS.

What is SELF?

The Atman, then, the highest 'principle' in man, is not his.
Though called the SELF for convenience, it is not my self or
yours, any more than the electric light in the lamp belongs to
that lamp. Yet in a sense it is this SELF which is the actor
whom we seek, albeit it acts without acting, without reactions,
without motive or result. For it uses the Self, if we may so

37

describe the principle of Enlightenment in every man, to the extent that the Self succeeds in freeing itself from the limitations of the personality, the Skandhas of Buddhist doctrine, the perishable components of the fleeting, untrue self. When the true actor acts, the actor, the means and the end coincide, but we are none of us yet at the level when the Buddhic- or Christ-principle within, the voice of Tao, the 'Essence of Mind' of the Patriarch Hui-neng which Dr Suzuki has called 'the suchness of the heart', is the actor day by day. Yet only when this SELF, 'existing alike imperishable in all perishable things' as described in the *Bhagavad Gita*, becomes the true actor, can there be the perfect act. For us this actor works through the karmic law of cause/effect on the lower planes, guided in right action by the voice, when it is obeyed, of Buddhi, the intuition. But for most of us the actor is at best at the level of Self, and all too often dominated and controlled by self which, though clearly seen as illusion, is powerful still.

What, then, if not the SELF, is this thing that you and I call 'I'? It is clearly extremely complex. It has been examined metaphysically, theologically, philosophically, psychologically, psychically, physiologically and biologically, and few can know what factor is at any one moment in control of this highly elaborate entity.

The Self and the self

This 'I' has been analysed at length in many ways, two of which are those recorded in the Theravada school of Buddhism, whose Scriptures were written down in the first century B.C., and in modern Western psychology. Both, in their several limited fields, agree to ignore the SELF as beyond the scope of scientific enquiry, and both agree that the human mind as we know it is at least twofold, here described as the higher and lower self, or Self and self. The main difference between the two analyses lies in the meaning of the unconscious, in the West a term of psychology, and in the East a term of metaphysics or philosophy. But they agree above all on the doctrine of Anatta. This teaching, rightly regarded as central to the vast field of thought known as Buddhism, has been in my view gravely misunderstood in the West, partly from mistranslation and partly because the earliest sponsers of Buddhism for the West were those of the Theravada school which interprets the doctrine in a way for which there is no scriptural foundation. In the early days of Western Buddhism it was called 'no-soul', but as no two students are agreed on the meaning of 'soul' this was not very helpful. It was, indeed, misleading for it led to the teaching that Buddhism denies the existence of any self whatsoever, permanent or temporary, in man or in the Universe, manifest or unmanifest. The average Englishman, a most sensible person, quite rightly rejected any such teaching as being entirely contrary to all his experience, to reason and to the deeper levels of his spiritual being. The word means non-*attā* or *atman*, and the doctrine states that there is in man no Atman which is his. Clearly there is not, or instead of an Absolute which becomes the One and the Many there would be an infinity of the Many each independently absolute, and this is a belief incompatible with any of the world's religions, with science, psychology and common sense. For myself I accepted, when I first read it at the age of seventeen, the summary of the late Dr Ananda Coomaraswamy in his greatest work, *Buddha and the Gospel of Buddhism*, (p. 199). There is nothing, he says, 'to show that the Buddhists ever really understood the pure doctrine of the Atman, which is "not so, not so" [*neti, neti*]. The attack which they led upon the idea of soul or self is directed against the conception of the eternity in time of an unchanging individuality; of the timeless spirit they do not speak, and yet they claim to have disposed of the theory of the Atman! In reality both sides were in agreement that the soul or ego (Manas, Ahamkara, Vijnana, etc.) is complex and phenomenal, while of that which is "not so" we know nothing.' That is plain enough, but if it be thought that this writer may be biased towards his native Hinduism, here is Dr D. T. Suzuki, a Japanese Buddhist of international standing. 'We can distinguish two phases of the ego-idea. The first is relative, psychological, empirical. The second is the transcendental ego.' And again, 'The denial of Atman as maintained by earlier Buddhists refers to Atman as the relative ego and not to the absolute ego, the ego after enlightenment—experience.'[1]

Note that Dr Coomaraswamy speaks of Buddhists and not of

[1] *Mysticism, Christian and Buddhist*, pp. 129 and 47.

the Buddha as not understanding the Atman. The Buddha himself according to the Scriptures expressly refused to say anything at all about the Self, much less the SELF. On these he maintained 'a noble silence', for whatever is said about them is apt to be misleading. To the man of action what matters is that the 'I' which loudly claims attention, which fights all day for its own advancement and harder still for its own survival, is not only unreal but the cause of suffering.

How, then, did this illusion arise? Again, it does not matter beyond the ambit of our present purpose, but as Alan Watts points out, 'The power of thought enables us to construct symbols of things apart from the things themselves. This includes the ability to make a symbol, an idea of ourselves apart from ourselves. Because the symbol is so much more stable than the fact we learn to identify ourselves with our idea of ourselves.'[1] Psychiatrists know how this dichotomy leads, when wide enough, to a mental breakdown, and in all of us it is the source of unnecessary tension. 'Before you can become extraordinary', a friend of mine was fond of saying, 'you must learn to become extra ordinary.' How many of us are willing to do that? Yet so long as we insist on discriminating between ourselves and the people and things around us we shall live in this world of false duality, and must suffer the results of the delusion. If the Absolute manifests as the One, and this One is the life that moves in all forms, then all that we know is the product of All-Mind, and there is no other mind that is separate from it. Nor is this only the teaching of the Orient. As Sir James Jeans wrote, 'The old dualism of mind and matter seems likely to disappear, not through matter becoming in any way more shadowy or insubstantial than before, or through mind becoming resolved into a function of the working of matter, but through substantial matter resolving itself into a creation and manifestation of mind.'[2] This is pure Buddhism, and applies to the whole constituents of our being. 'All that we are', says the *Dhammapada*, the most famous of Buddhist Scriptures, 'is the result of what we have thought; it is founded on our thoughts and made up of our thoughts.' Or in the words of the Patriarch Hui-neng of China in the seventh century A.D., 'Our Essence

[1] *The Way of Zen*, pp. 119-20.   [2] *The Mysterious Universe*, p. 137.

of Mind is intrinsically pure; all things are only its manifestations, and good deeds and evil deeds are only the result of
good thoughts and evil thoughts respectively.'

The habitual 'I'

The habitual 'I', then, can be pulled to pieces and found to
contain no abiding entity. Yet it exists, and to refuse to give it,
as a provisional and changing thing, a provisional and temporary name is a purism which does not help. So long as we
remember that it is neither immortal nor 'mine' the word
'soul', which St Paul placed between Spirit and body, is as
good a term as any. Meanwhile let us briefly take it to pieces,
or we shall not understand its complex aims and methods, its
motivation, internal conflicts and inability, save on rare occasions, to act as a single unit, from the SELF that is inexpressible
down to the hands that do the deed. The East has a large
variety of classifications, basically sevenfold, but frequently less
for practical purposes. St Paul was content with three, body,
soul and spirit, and for most of us this is sufficient. Analogies
help but none can be taken too far. I favour my own, the lighthouse, for while it has the Light at the top which is not its own
light, it is based on the rock, and the keeper, representing
consciousness, moves at will on the various levels between. But
whether this simile be used, or that of the onion which can be
unpeeled and unpeeled till there is nothing left, we begin with
the body, the body without which we are not alive and which
alone is visible to most of us.

The Constituents of Self

This body must perish and die, and indeed it begins to die as
soon as it is born. In Buddhist parlance, 'the cause of death is
birth'. It is the physical-plane instrument of the Self or self
which uses it, and should be so trained and used. Within it,
or 'above' it if we use the lighthouse simile, is the etheric body,
of a finer degree of physical matter, visible to some, and above
this is the astral, to adopt the Theosophical term, though it has
other names in other systems of thought. This is the true home
of the five senses; it is the ghost seen by those of psychic vision
and, more important, it is the seat of the emotions which, by

Eastern teaching, are forces emanating from a centre as distinct from the physical as from the mental plane. These emotions, of love/hate, fear and the like, work down into the physical body and affect its nervous and glandular reactions, as with fear, sexual excitement or anger; and upward into the thought-machine or 'lower mind', where the calm of thought may be violently disturbed by emotion, good or bad. To the psychic with vision on this plane, emotion rises as a cloud and literally impedes clear thinking, and an angry or frightened man cannot achieve dispassionate judgment.

So to the lower mind or thinking apparatus, a machine which may be powerful or weak, developed or undeveloped, under control or acting entirely by reflex to outside stimuli. This is the apparatus we use in the thousand situations of the day which call for analysis and synthesis, choice and judgment. It works by concepts or thought-forms, which are fragments of life, so to speak, encased in labelled boxes as opinions, conclusions, principles, beliefs, 'ideas about', and plans for the future. It is in these that we enshrine remembrance of an actual experience, of direct awareness either of the outer world or the higher Truth. When I put my hand on something very hot I jump with pain. That is a direct experience. My memory of it, anger at it, chatter about it, are second-hand, and no longer direct experience, and the words I use to describe the experience are themselves but concepts or symbols in sound of thoughts which are also second-hand. A flash of intuitive realization is also direct experience, but we remember it, talk about it and record it through the use of concepts, the second-hand bricks of thought by which we build communication and enshrine discovery. More of this later when we come to mind-development, but although the self is one though complex, it is well to appreciate the separate functions of its parts. A car is a car as a unit, but it is well, if you wish to look after it, to appreciate the difference between the magneto and the gear-box.

All these 'bodies' die at the death of the Rupa or physical vehicle, and may be collated with the first four of the Skandhas of early Buddhist doctrine. These are Rupa or body, Vedana, sense reactions to contact, Sanna, perceptions of these reactions, and the Samkharas, usually called mental predispositions, which include all the factors of character karmically produced by past action, and all our memories, regrets, ambitions, abilities and limitations and ideals. The fifth of these five is consciousness, but if the lighthouse analogy be right, it is impossible to confine this factor at any point, for in the developed man it may function where he pleases.

So to the 'higher mind', a useful term to denote a difference which we all admit to exist. This is the world of synthesis as distinct from analysis, of wider vision, of ideals. At this height man may be seen as a unit, and the higher ranges of each department of human acting may be reached and their interrelation seen. On this plane work the greatest scientists, musicians, thinkers, religious leaders and the leaders of mankind in every sphere of noble activity.

The Intuition
But the greatness of the higher mind, the factor which illumines it and makes it the Self which is capable of Enlightenment, is Buddhi, the intuition, the highest factor in any man which he can claim as 'his'. This is the spark of the flame, the reflection of the Light, the ray of the sun's light in the house of the mind, the faculty in man which enables him, as the result of direct experience of the One, to say I KNOW. This is the plane of our being which, as the Buddha within, is, as Professor Murti says, 'amphibious, having one foot in the Absolute and the other in phenomena. And it is because of this that he performs the function of a mediator between the two.'[1]

The higher mind illumined by the intuition is the noblest aspect of man, and as the Light grows he approaches Enlightenment. This is the Self which should be in control of the total man, but whose activities and progress are impeded hour by hour by the passions, selfishness and blindness of the self. It is not surprising, then, that all religions are at one in attacking the self which clouds the vision of the God within, though Buddhism is the only Way which has made the illusionary nature of this self its central doctrine.

Above Buddhi is nothing which belongs to the individual.

[1] T. R. V. Murti: *The Central Philosophy of Buddhism* (Allen & Unwin 1955), p. 284.

There is but Atman, the ray of the Absolute which, through the vehicle of Buddhi, is the light of life in the complex unit called a man. Of this nothing can be said, and the Buddha refused to attempt to say it.

So much for a brief analysis, to be gleaned from the vast range of Buddhist teaching by any man for himself, but the man remains a whole man, and more than a collection of parts. The lighthouse is a unit, and the light would not shine if the base itself were not part of it. Yet at every point the basic duality may be seen, spirit descending into matter and matter returning into spirit. The complexity of parts and the subtlety of inter-relationship are almost unbelievable, yet when the 'rolling up' of the universe is again complete, each part of the whole, purified of the last defilement, will return to the Unmanifest, made richer, we must presume, by its long 'day' of experience.

For working purposes, then, we can adopt the triple man of self, the arch-enemy of Theravada Buddhism, Self, the Buddhi-illumined changing, progressing, bundle of attributes which moves to Enlightenment, and the SELF about which nothing can be said at all. The first is selfish, the second unselfish, the third selfless in any shape or form. The first acts from wrong motive, seeking to enlarge its own importance, the second from right motive, the advancement of the weal of the whole; the third is motiveless. The first claims too much of our consciousness; the second more and more becomes I; the third is the supreme Unconscious which to our understanding is coterminous with Absolute Consciousness.

Western Psychology

Faced, then, with a basically dual self, and the need for the higher to dominate and cleanse the lower, we turn to the helpful yet complicating discoveries of Western psychology. Buddhism had its own developed system of psychology two thousand years ago, and not much later it was written down. It is available in English today, but the West ignores these old discoveries, and basing its new analysis of thought on the newly-discovered psychological unconscious, has produced its own crop of 'selves'. The psyche, the ego, the super-ego and the Id have now to be collated with Eastern thought, though here is not the place to attempt it. We hear of self-suppression, self-repression, self-expression and much beside, but we also hear of psycho-somatic medicine, which admits the extremely close relation between body and mind. Two healers, Dr Laurence Bendit and his wife, Phoebe Payne, have bravely attempted in two books[1] to write of the psychic plane in terms of western medicine, and C. G. Jung himself, in *The Secret of the Golden Flower* has laid the foundations of a bridge between Eastern and Western spiritual principles on which others may be skilful enough to build. But Western psychology will not come into its own until it lifts the concrete roof which it has firmly built over its head. Dr Graham Howe, himself attempting to follow on the heels of Jung, points out, 'The structure of "scientific" psychology is only a matter of form, an abstraction from a limiting point of view. Psychology does not reveal to us the whole truth about the person of the patient. In fact it must obscure it, unless we can see through psychology to the spiritual problem.'[2] For the total self is vast in range as in complexity, and any single part of it, or the relationship between two parts, may go sick. Even the unconscious must sooner or later be synthesized with that tiny lighted ring in the illimitable darkness, and the two, the conscious and unconscious, unified and transcended in a total acceptance which dominates and absorbs them. This new Self, which Jung says grows at the intersection of the two, and Suzuki says is born at a point which is at once within and without the experience of Satori, is the birth of the Self which, having digested a purified self, looks upward to its own divinity, the Whole of which it is part and yet, in ecstasy of raised awareness, the very whole.

There are other factors in man which need not here detain us. The allied concepts of motive, purpose and intent, the will, and conscience which, like motive, varies in nature according to the plane on which it functions, these may be reviewed later. For the moment we have a working difference of a Self and a self, and the relationship is clear. In the words of the *Dhammapada*, 'Self is the Lord of self and the goal of self. What other Lord can there be?'

But although each self is extremely complex there are

---

[1] *The Psychic Sense*, and *This World and That*.
[2] *Mysterious Marriage*, p. 246.

definite psychological types, and it is right to note their existence in deciding right action for ourselves and right judgment of our fellow men. Jung's famous diagram of the four types is now well known, the intellect and the emotions being on two sides of his diagram, with intuition and sensation at the top and bottom. In each of these pairs, he says, one factor is dominant, and the other, for want of adequate expression is apt to remain suppressed and to cause trouble. Intellect and emotion are complementary parts of the mind to digest direct experience, and in each of us one or the other is the more developed. The other pair have this in common, that each is an organ of direct experience, sensation for the physical plane and the intuition for the plane of direct awareness, of contact with Reality.

To this classification, which is capable of much sub-division, Jung has added the complementary pair of the extroverts and the introverts, the former being turned outwards, and his energies conditioned by the object; the latter having his energy turned inwards, towards the subject. These are as clearly complementary as male and female bodies, and no man is purely either. Other classifications are legion. In England we talk of the Puritan and the Cavalier, the 'go-getter' and the dreamer, while astrology, whatever its uses for fortune-telling, is extremely valuable in typing the person's character, even differentiating between the personality and the deeper individuality, a distinction which we all know from experience. The two schools of Buddhism, the Theravada and the Mahayana, are also in my view to be distinguished as a psychological 'pair of opposites', and it is often easy to suggest to a certain type of new-comer into the field of Buddhism which of the schools will be more likely to satisfy his needs.

Seeing that in the house of self there are so many voices advocating different ways of action, there is at all times a bitter and remorseless war within. Bishop Blougram, through his author, Robert Browning, puts it best:

'When the fight begins within himself
A man's worth something. God stoops o'er his head,
Satan looks up between his feet—both tug—
He's left, himself, in the middle: the soul wakes
And grows. Prolong that battle through his life!'

Until the battle of self is won all talk of peace within is a mischievous and idle dream. 'Warriors, warriors, Lord, we call ourselves. In what way are we warriors?' 'We wage war, O Bhikkhus; therefore are we called warriors.' 'Wherefore, Lord, do we wage war?' 'For lofty virtue, for high endeavour, for sublime wisdom—for these things do we wage war, O Bhikkhus; therefore are we called warriors.'

This is no casual struggle but a whole-time job, and after a while it is found to be the only thing worth doing. But this inner war, when magnified by millions, spills over into outward action and produces warfare between men. For while there is no peace within, and men look outward for the causes of war, there can be no peace in the world. The cause of all war is a projection of the struggle in every mind, between higher and lower, better and worse, into the world of affairs, and it will cease when that battle is won. Self is the cause of the war within; a million selves the cause of war without. War will end when that illusion dies within; the price of peace is self.

Meanwhile the warrior makes Karma in his struggle and returns to life again and again to reap its consequences. He makes Karma, in the sense of producing causes for which he must suffer the effects, by means of his wrong action. Let us look briefly at some of his wrong acts, that we may learn to act better on our long road to the best.

Chapter 3

Wrong Action

*There are two ways of doing anything; the right
way and the wrong way.*   TRADITIONAL

Only the skilled thing is good.   PHIROZ MEHTA

BUDDHISTS say that all wrong action arises from Avidya,
ignorance, unawareness of the truth of things, lack of Awakening. When we are truly awakened, that is, enlightened and
made one with our own essential nature of Non-duality, we
shall be rid of our ignorance, and in this new-found 'seeing' pass
beyond the sway of the opposites, including those of good and
evil. But not until. For these are inherent in the manifest
universe. So soon as the One became Two good and evil were
born; when these Two disappear, so will the pair with which
we are here concerned. We cannot know good, and therefore
cannot discover the Good, unless evil exists to show the
difference. Ultimately all will be Well, and there was intuition
in Thoreau's famous claim: 'I know that the enterprise is
worthy. I know that things work well; I have heard no bad
news.' Meanwhile we must face this false duality, so real in
the world of the relative, for it contains the secret of all wrong
action.

Good and bad as labels
But we must drop the habit of labelling. 'Nothing is good or
bad but thinking makes it so', and what in one way is right
action is in another wrong; the rightness or wrongness of any
event is largely a matter of projected opinion. To use an old
analogy, rain is rain and as such neither good nor bad. Yet to
the man who needs it for his crops it is good and for the hostess
with a garden party on hand the same rain is bad. Epictetus put

it well:—' "His son is dead." "What has happened?" "His son is dead." "His ship is lost." "What has happened?" "His ship is lost." "He has been haled to prison." "What has happened?" "He has been haled to prison." "Nothing more?" "Nothing more." But that any of these things are misfortune to him, is an addition which every man makes of his own.'

But this is not deep enough. There is evil in the world that not even a Stoic can ignore, and we must face the conflict between such evil and its opposite good. This conflict, which a Buddhist scripture calls the sickness of the mind, is to us real, and we cannot escape from it. Meanwhile we must have criteria for deciding what, in any situation, is good, what evil. The fulcrum must be the One; it can be no other. True, greater than oneness is THAT which is non-dual, being beyond the One and the Many. But once the One became many, this very separation gave birth to the sense of evil. It follows that all is right which moves towards oneness, synthesis, reunion, and all is evil which separates or perpetuates separation. All that hurts another part of the whole is evil unless the harming be to heal; all that helps the littlest mode of life in its journey 'home' is good. It may be that evil must be done for the good of a greater unity, that men must be imprisoned lest they do more harm to their fellows. But how much action is by this criterion seen to be wrong, however hallowed by custom or regarded today as right? Our social system, any social system, must be full of wrong when it has to allow for the utterly differing needs and desires of the million, be they good, bad or indifferent, and to synthesize them into the greatest good for the whole. But for the individual in his private life, or the individual striving to do right in the governance of his fellow men, there can surely be no better criterion than this:—Does the act contemplated tend to aid or hinder the cosmic tendencies as we perceive them, to move from the many to One, or to increase the fragmentation of the Many? Because there is so much action which has the latter result it may be worth while to examine it.

Wrong action may take place on any plane. Most physical action is thought-prompted, but there may be physical acts which are in themselves wrong, and the cause should be traced. More serious are the wrong desires which manifest in the desire or astral body, the seat of the emotions. For desire is subtly linked with the will. It is the steering wheel of the self as a whole, and decides the direction in which the total unit of self is at the moment moving. Will may be the horse-power of the vehicle, but there is an ancient saying, 'Behind will stands desire', and when the desire is based in the self the whole man may be led, with huge momentum and therefore enormous consequences, off the road of the Middle Way and over the precipice. Nor will a 'good' desire be always right. Eckhart speaks of those who are 'yoked to their affections', and love, so called, may be grossly and blindly selfish. This element of desire, when attached to self, is a powerful ingredient in motive, but motive is also a creature of thought and thought-habit, and may be considered later.

Wrong action in the mind

Wrong action by the mind is no man's monopoly, for until the final Awakening each thinking entity will wrongly think and suffer the consequences. Here we are primarily concerned with the Western mind, which is more analytic, intellectual and extrovert, to the East's more intuitive and inward approach to Reality. Our Western mind is concept-ridden to a degree that few of its victims realize. With our values projected onto outside things we are bound by the values that we give them, and our principles, convictions, conclusions, opinions, plans and ideals decide not only our actions but largely why we do them. The analytic power of the intellect is perhaps the West's contribution to the culture and total advancement of mankind, but if it is the Western thinker's friend it is at the same time his most subtle enemy. For it blocks the way to further advance-ment, and many of our finest intellects quite seriously believe that it is man's ultimate possession, that by its aid he will sooner or later contact Reality. But the intellect, the machine of thought, is bound by duality, and the complementary concepts which are the bricks of thought which go to build a conclusion or principle. The intellect cannot know; it can only know more and more about. Sooner or later thought must be transcended, and to some extent transcended by its own process. Only by finer and finer and more 'right' thinking will the intuition be roused to see the 'suchness of things', and the Light within be allowed to shine.

But the finest thought cannot function accurately when clouded with emotion. We cannot think straight—an interesting word in this connection—if we are pulled off the straight or Middle Way by like or dislike and its forces of self-craving, animosity and fear. When desire, conscious or sub-conscious, wants a decision to be this or that, how can the intellect dispassionately choose? Yet how often will a member of an audience, first faced, for example, with the doctrine of Karma, or of the omnipresence of change and the non-existence of security, cry out, 'But I don't like such a law. I refuse to believe in that'! But the emotional valuation of like/dislike is quite distinct from the intellect's view that it is true or untrue, and to the thinking mind the emotional reaction to a proposition is utterly irrelevant.

Meanwhile, until the intuition is developed and allowed to speak, we muddle thinking with feeling, and are far from the true motive for all action which should be based on reason and the experience behind it. Ultimately we must learn to be motiveless, and to allow the irrational because super-rational force of No-mind to direct our actions. Until then we must suffer from our thinking, however right, and still more from the thoughts which are the product of Avidya, ignorance. Even our best principles may suffer from being too rigid, as shown in the delicious story of Chuang-Tzu, the successor of Lao-Tzu in the field of Taoism. 'A keeper of monkeys said with regard to their ration of chestnuts that each was to have three in the morning and four at night. At this the monkeys were very angry, so the keeper said they could have four in the morning and three at night; with which arrangement they were well pleased. This was an adaptation to the likes and dislikes of those concerned. . . .' We rail at petty officials who cling to the letter of the law as given them, but are we less deplorable in our refusal to vary our own pet habits, physical or mental?

Escapism

Strangely enough, the most persistent of our wrong thought-habits is the habit of running away, of refusing to face a fact that frightens us, or that we do not wish to admit from feelings of shame. And one of the facts that frightens us most is Truth, the truth that we loudly claim to be seeking. It offends our present-held ideas, our self-esteem or our ambition, and so we run. We escape into societies or religions, into slogans, phrases and 'new ideas', into pleasure, hobbies and distractions, into prayer to an outside Force to which we give the power to 'save' us, whatever that may mean. Or we escape into illness, or madness, or even death. We will not face what we have done, nor find out why we did it. So we project the entire performance onto an outside cause. We blame the weather, the government, the boss or even the abstract cussedness of things that we are apt to label 'they'. We refuse to withdraw these futile efforts to escape, and so deprive ourselves of the opportunity to learn from the consequences of the experience. It is therefore wise to analyse those actions which we secretly deplore, and to find the cause of them. We may lie to our friends as to motive and even deny what is done, but it is surely foolish to lie, as we do, to ourselves. Yet when the error and its cause are clearly seen the cure begins to follow. I have not found in my own life or in those of my friends that there is need for self-imposed and rigid rules of conduct. When error is truly seen as such the desire for it begins to fade, and a bad habit so acknowledged is half-way to being dropped. Nine tenths of the wrongs we commit are not thought to be right, but are done because we will not admit to ourselves that they are wrong. I love to quote Gerald Gould in this:—

'For God's sake, if you sin, take pleasure in it,
  And do it for the pleasure.' Do not say:
'Behold the spirit's liberty!—a minute
  Will see the earthly vesture break away
And God shine through.' Say: 'Here's a sin—I'll sin it;
  And there's the price of sinning—and I'll pay'!

Four headings of wrong action

The wrongness of our present action, apart from evil deliberately done which is, for most of us, comparatively rare, falls under four headings. The first is sheer feebleness of decision, motive, means and execution. Whatever the cause, whether lack of will-power, lack of precision of thought, doubts about rightness, indecision about means, we all know the ineffectiveness of our neighbour's actions and our own. As said in the *Bhagavad Gita*, 'The man of doubtful mind hath no happiness in this world or the next.' There is a very old saying that 'Nature spews the lukewarm from her mouth'; as well known in the East is the saying of the Zen Master Ummon to his pupils, 'If you walk, just walk. If you sit just sit, but don't wobble.' It is useless for a splendid car to be faced in the right direction if it so lacks power that a puff of wind will stop it. We think that we think rightly. Can we even think? We glibly say to our friends, 'I think . . .', but it is seldom true. Have we come to a precise judgment on all available evidence, and after a definite process of deep thinking come to a conclusion which will stand up to rational analysis? Very seldom! Even our vaunted consciousness is hard-earned and hardly held. Much of our lives we are quite unconscious, and much of our waking life is spent in such vague day-dreaming that we are at best half-conscious of the world about us.

The second heading for wrong action is waste. The horsepower of our present car is limited; so is the quantity of petrol (or spirit, and the pun is justified) available to run it. Not yet can we 'attach our belt to the power-house of the universe', as Ralph Waldo Trine advised, and have unlimited power at our command. Yet we run the engine all day, go useless journeys here and there, and waste available energy on every plane. With our physical bodies we fidget incessantly, and a Zen abbot once told me that the outstanding feature of his Western visitors was that they could not keep still. It has been said of Winston Churchill that the secret of his ability to work intensely for long hours was his power of complete relaxation at will, and the fact that he never made an unnecessary movement. Our emotional waste is even greater, and we react to outside stimuli with like or dislike, worry, hope and fear to an extent we cannot believe until we develop the strength and skill to analyse that reaction. To the psychic the emotional aura of the average man can be seen in a constant state of violent vibration, and we worry, which is a form of fear, at a thousand situations which call for no such force to be expended. A man may enter a room and give his friends an item of news. The response is like a flock of birds at rest when the hands are clapped loudly. What a pother! How horrible, how gorgeous, how disgraceful, what fun, is the reaction, followed by immediate suggestions for action, all alike uncalled for in that the matter is no concern whatever of the persons present. No wonder, then, that those emotionally inclined are indeed exhausted at the end of the day, with no available energy for the task which needs all the energy at command.

More difficult still to master is the habit which Phiroz Mehta in a memorable phrase called 'mental chattering'. Of what use to keep the lips sealed if the mind is raging about its cage of concept with silent nagging, criticism, spiteful comparisons and muttered self-defence. How much of our energy goes in day-dreams, devised with a wealth of imagination which might be better spent on a novel or a stage production. And when they begin with the thought, as many do, 'If only . . .', to waste of energy is added an evil form of escapism. For this is a rank refusal to face facts, to face things as they are. More, it exhibits the foolish belief that were circumstances different 'I' should be able to do what I cannot now. This is a lie, for if 'I' were different my circumstances would be different, but a change in the facts about me will not of itself change me.

As a third heading for wrong action, much of our wasted energy comes from lack of control of reaction to outside happenings, and few in fact appreciate how much of their action is thus produced. Watch the mind on a journey. Watch its reaction to advertisements, passers by, the incidents around. It is not that we should be icicles, or lumps of stone, but we must sooner or later learn to control our reactions at will. The man who is 'mindful and self-possessed' can enjoy the pleasures of this illusory world at will, but he chooses from the spate of thoughts and emotions which move in procession through his mind those on which he will spend some portion of his energy. The rest flow through.

Allied to this form of wrong effort is a fourth, our habit of interfering where we should not interfere, and remaining passive, from laziness or fear or ignorance, when there is right work to be done. The relative error equates with the basic types of the extrovert and the introvert. The former acts too often, the latter remains passive and is at fault with such inaction. The comparison applies to the complementary goals of the Theravada and Mahayana Buddhist, whose respective ideals are the Arhat, concerned with his own enlightenment, and the Bodhisattva, concerned alone with the salvation of all mankind. In the West we are encouraged to be 'good neighbours' and to appreciate the virtues of social service. The East is more concerned with minding its own business, and leaving its neighbour to mind his. In each case the exception is frowned on by the multitude. The Easterner who turned to social reform was at first an outcast from the herd, the man who would not leave well alone; in the West the individual who wishes to remain as such, 'working out his own salvation' as enjoined by the Buddha, is looked at askance by his friends, who are so busy telling their neighbours how to conduct their lives that they have no energy to improve their own.

These are but four of the manifold forms of wrongdoing. The cause of them all is self, its laziness, its wasteful dissipation of energy in pursuit of new attractions, its wilful interference for its own advantage. All spring from ignorance, from the false belief that its interests can be served at the expense of others, its pathetic illusion that it exists at all and is other than an obstruction in the cosmic scheme of things.

Motive

When an act is deliberate, with the means planned to a clearly envisaged end, we may well consider the motive behind it. English criminal law makes a clear distinction between the *mens rea* or guilty mind and the *actus reus* or wicked act, and in most cases both are needed to make an offence complete. As motive works on the plane of thought it is far more important in the occult field than the mere act, which may be the result of error or accident, or be merely thoughtless. Here we must distinguish motive or purpose from intent, to see that either or both may be wrong in any one act. When a man goes burgling his intent is usually clear, to steal. But what moved him, for that is the meaning of motive, the force that moved him from rest to go into action? It might be greed but it might be to get money for food for his children. It might be revenge on society for the way it used him as a child; it might be a desire to show off to his fellows that he is able to carry out daring crimes and to get away with it. For most of us motive is mixed good and bad. At the lowest it is the creation of self; later it adds the element of thought for others and is reasonably unselfish. Only a long way towards the Goal shall we learn to 'tarry forever in purposelessness'. Meanwhile we can aim at the ideal of the *Bhagavad Gita*. 'Let, then, the motive for action be in the action itself, and not in the event.' If this is still too hard, at least we can learn to examine motive, a habit which the Englishman, according to H. G. Baynes, is slow to acquire. He seldom knows his own mind, he says, 'not because he is inordinately given to psychological masquerade, but rather on account of the persuasive extraverted mental habit of representing reality in terms of self-evident goals instead of inquiring into motives'.[1] He prefers to make the act itself, which he regards as right because it is the usual thing to do, sufficient motive for continuing to do it. 'The goal which the Englishman erects and the path that he follows, have for him the character of self-evident validity, not because they are the product of profound reflection, but because they emerge as the obvious, practical, commonsense things to be done.'[2] But this is the voice of the herd. The individual member of it will never begin the road to wholeness, to Self-possession, until he forms the motive for every act from his inner processes, regardless of the approval or disapproval of the herd. A man must walk the path of his own choosing, and it is useless if it leads him wrong, or nowhere, to complain that it is trodden by all the other members of his club.

Causes of Suffering

Thus there is wrong action everywhere, from murder to an unkind word, from a lustful thought to rape, from failure to pay the correct bus fare to robbing the Bank of England. The doers are made unhappy, for this alone have criminals in common, that they are unhappy people until they have paid the price of the deed. And those who are never labelled criminals but who

[1] *Analytical Psychology and the English Mind*, p. 34.
[2] *Ibid.*

do what they know is wrong are sad to the limits of their avowed wrong-doing. They suffer because they acted at the behest of self; and they gave way to the desires of self, either because the desire was beyond the control of the Self or because they still believed that the self of their desires existed as a separate entity.

With suffering and its omnipresence we are only here concerned to the extent that it is a spur to right action and a curb on wrong. That it is the consequence of a large proportion of our actions should be noted, as also of our reaction to the acts of others. But we truly suffer from ourselves.

> 'Ye suffer from yourselves. None else compels,
> None other holds you that ye live and die,
> And whirl upon the wheel, and hug and kiss
> Its spokes of agony . . .'[1]

And the cause of the suffering is self. Where self exists there is suffering; where there is suffering there is a self to suffer. To remove suffering, therefore, slay the self, or let it die as a fire dies for want of fuelling. The end of self is the criterion of Enlightenment, and such was the Buddha's cry when he achieved it.

> 'But now,
> Thou Builder of the Tabernacle—Thou!
> I know thee! Never shalt thou build again
> These walls of pain,
> Nor raise the roof-tree of deceits, nor lay
> Fresh rafters on the clay;
> Broken thy house is, and the ridge-pole split!
> Delusion fashioned it!
> Safe pass I thence—deliverance to attain.'[2]

How? How do we break the ridge-pole of the house of self? Not in an hour or a single life-time, but by treading a Way, described in the utmost detail by one who trod it to the end, the Buddha's Way to Enlightenment. These are the Four Noble Truths of Buddhism. Fully understood there is little more to

---

[1] From the eighth book of the *Light of Asia* by Sir Edwin Arnold.
[2] *Ibid.*

learn, but for most of us the Way is scarce begun, and every wrong act is a deviation from the Way which involves, first, a return to it at the point of departure, secondly, suffering as the consequence and thirdly, unhappiness as the result of the suffering entailed.

Meanwhile we suffer in our ignorance for the wrong acts we perform, all of which, we shall discover, fall to one side or the other of a widthless Middle Way.

Chapter 4

The Actor and his Circumstance

If any man be unhappy, let him know that it is by reason of himself alone.　　　EPICTETUS

IF the One, after its emanation from THAT, became, in the illusion of time, the Many, then each of the Many is necessary to the One. The individual, therefore, as a unit of the Many, is a unit of development. The totality may have its own progress, from spirit to matter and back again in 'the unrolling and rolling up of the worlds', but in Kipling's words, 'the race is run by one and one and never by two and two'. There can be no salvation by one unit of another, although the example of others, and their 'accumulated merit', in the phrase of the Mahayana, is ever at the service of the least member of the brotherhood of life. Indeed there are those who regard the Mahayana's shift of emphasis from self-discipline to altruism as a shift for the worse. 'Such a concession to human sentiment was disastrous. No man could help his fellow save by the force of his example, save by the spectacle of his achieved holiness.'[1] In spiritual affairs the man is always more important than the tribe or state, or that vague entity, 'mankind'. All doctrine which elevates the State at the expense of the individual is evil; it reverses the current of good. The well-trained individual, man, woman or child, is the only true objective of civilization, for a nation of such is the ideal state. A developed and independent man is of more use to the nation than a frightened slave, and the worship of the concept of a state is to create a devil within whose grip the flower of spirit dies.

Yet the individual does not live on a desert island; he is part of a whole.

[1] L. H. Myers: *The Root and the Flower*, p. 27.

The Nature of Circumstance

As such he must be aware of and will react to his circumstance, which is collectively those things, visible or invisible, which 'stand around' the thing he knows as self. They stand around SELF even as the universe is the temporary circumstance of THAT, and may be considered in concentric rings of ever wider radius. About the SELF, which is no man's, is the Self, the ever-changing character which the Theravadin Buddhists rightly describe as Anatta, having no permanent, separate existence. About Self and its vehicles, including its physical body, are the man's relations and friends, his home, job and hobbies, his possessions, tangible and mental, including all that the world accords him of honour and prestige. Wider still is the circle of his class and caste, and beyond that his race and nation. About that lies the earth and all that dwells therein, and the whole universe on its seven planes. To nearly all these 'things' we add labels. We seek to classify, distinguish, evaluate; to make clear what we like or dislike, of what we approve and of what, often in ignorance but no less loudly, we disapprove.

Yet all of circumstance, not some of it, must be fairly faced. There is no escape from it, any more than we can escape from our character. It is changing from moment to moment, and all attempts at security are waste of time. We can insure that we shall be given the thing called money to replace some other article destroyed by fire; we cannot, by signing any document, ensure that our homes and jobs and neighbours will not change increasingly, and the only wisdom, as Alan Watts wrote a book to prove,[1] is contented insecurity. We must develop trust in the God-within, the Buddha-within, in the Essence of Mind which is 'intrinsically pure'. We shall not starve in the process, and in our walking on will be free from so much attachment to our circumstance.

All of it is soulless, even as we; that is, in its change it reveals an absence of any factor not the subject of birth and death. For, as already pointed out, we change as fast as our circumstance. All speculation, therefore, on what we should do if we could live our life again, or what we shall do when this and that shall happen, is idle and vain. For we shall be different

[1] *The Wisdom of Insecurity.*

when those things come to pass; therefore we shall react differently. It is useless to say of a friend, 'If I were he I would do so and so.' You would not; if you were he you would do what he does. There is an old saying that no man dips his pitcher into the same river twice. In the same way no man reads the same book twice, for the reader will be different.

But the most important factor about our circumstance is this, that we made it. In a later chapter on Action and Reaction this theme will be developed. For the moment it is stated as a fact that all about us is our circumstance because we made it so; it is the product of our own imagining. All manifestation is the child of Mind and matter, and the world of life and death is the product of that Mind, as assisted or confused by the thinking of its unit minds, ourselves. It can affect us as we give it power, not otherwise. The worst that any man can do to another is to bring forward the date of his death, and even that act is within the law of harmony, of cause/effect. Indeed, no circumstance can hurt a man save as he gives it leave, or has given it so freely that for the moment he must suffer the effects of that permission. Meanwhile, as Epictetus said, 'Anytus and Melitus may put me to death; to injure me is beyond their power.' And he quotes the famous saying of Heraclitus, who had a petty suit about a farm at Rhodes. He produced his evidence to show that his cause was just, then ended his speech by saying, 'I will not entreat you, nor do I care what judgment you pass. It is you who are on trial, not I.'

Already, then, the dual attitude to circumstance is beginning to appear. First we must understand it for what it is, with a view to changing it; then we must firmly decide our reaction to it. Of these the latter is far more important. We must set our own house in order before attempting to improve the chaos around. 'Though one conquer a thousand times a thousand men in battle, he who conquers himself is the greatest warrior.' And again, 'Better than sovereignty over the earth, better than the heaven-state, better than dominion over all the worlds is the first step on the Noble Eightfold Path' to self-dominion. Thus the *Dhammapada*, and all the scriptures of the world bear witness to the same dynamic principle.

We can use our energy to alter circumstance or to accept it.

'Ah Love! Could thou and I with Fate conspire
To grasp this sorry Scheme of Things entire,
Would we not shatter it to bits—and then
Re-mould it nearer to the Heart's desire.'

Thus Omar Khayyam, but the answer is clear; until the self
has been remoulded—to the point of extinction—all interference
with circumstance will not improve it nearer to the Heart's
Desire. First, then, let it be accepted; then change the subject
that the object may be altered for the better. Though the two
processes are one—'While moving and changing, one must
become the moving and changing'—yet here we are concerned with individual action, and therefore in the first place
with our reaction to circumstance rather than with the reform
of all mankind.

Subject and object

This involves a brief analysis of the subject/object relationship.
In the words of Rinzai, founder of the Rinzai school of Zen
Buddhism, there are four reactions to the two which indicate
an ascending comprehension of Enlightenment. One can negate
the subject and not the object; negate the object and not the
subject; deny both subject and object, and finally take away
neither subject nor object, thus affirming both.[1] This classification
revolves about the central vacuum or Void (Sunyata) which is
alone Reality.

> The object is an object for the subject,
> The subject is a subject for an object:
> Know that the relativity of the two
> Rests ultimately on the oneness of the Void.[2]

But as yet we are not capable of viewing subject and object
at the same time, and indeed, as Benoit says, 'When I think
that I have an intellectual knowledge of the outside world, I
only have knowledge of the modifications of my Self—in contact
with the outside world. Philosophers call that "the prison of
my subjectivity", disregarding my organic consciousness which

---

[1] Dumoulin and Sasaki: *The Development of Chinese Zen*, p. 22.
[2] Suzuki: *Essays in Zen Buddhism, First Series*, p. 184.

does not discriminate between subject and object and thanks to which I am already virtually free.'[1] But this 'organic consciousness' must be achieved. It springs from the union of the unconsciousness and conscious minds, which are aspects of a mind which is basically Mind-Only, but this balance, between an objective attitude to the universe and a subjective regard for the processes of life within, can only be acquired by practice, as indeed all else.

But at least the mind can attempt to grasp the nature of things in themselves, and see in each the element of Tathata, the 'suchness' or 'thusness' in all things, that which makes them what they are. 'God is an angel in an angel, a stone in a stone, and a straw in a straw', said John Donne. Eckhart went further. 'The man to whom God is dearer in one thing than another, that man is a barbarian, still in the wilds, a child. He to whom God is the same in everything has come to man's estate.' The *Tao Tê Ching*, which is older than either of these, makes the distinction which is without difference.

> 'Man is earth when conforming to earth,
> He is heaven when conforming to heaven,
> He is Tao when conforming to Tao.
> Let him thus conform himself to the suchness of things.'

If this is too subtle or metaphysical, G. K. Chesterton brought it to earth for us. 'I do not think there is anyone who takes quite such a fierce pleasure in things being themselves as I do. The startling wetness of water excites and intoxicates me; the fieriness of fire, the steeliness of steel, the unutterable muddiness of mud.'[2] Such is the suchness of all things and it is one with the Plenum/Void.

Attachment and detachment

The actor is linked with his environment by desire and attachment, and not all desire is wrong. Without it there would be no move towards Enlightenment, and the best within us does the best that we do from desire that is still part selfish, only reasonably 'right'. It is not desire that is the cause of suffering but

[1] *The Supreme Doctrine*, p. 180.
[2] Quoted in Gollancz: *A Year of Grace*, p. 85.

attachment to the objects of desire. Had we no passions, ambitions, powerful resolves, where were the force which, purged of self, would lead us to Awakening? Was it not desire that caused the universe to emerge from THAT? 'Behind will stands desire' is a very old saying, for desire is the direction given to will, the path to be followed, whether 'right' or 'wrong'. The stronger it is the stronger the force which, guided by Wisdom and not self, will travel the road from the Many back to the One. It is therefore not desire that is wrong, but choice of object of desire and the attachment to it. For attachment limits the subject, reduces the speed of his 'walking on', binds him in the dust of things when he would lift his wings and fly. Shadows are not made by the sun but by the object which hinders the light of the sun. 'Man stands in his own shadow and wonders why it is dark.' Attachment weakens, darkens the mind; it is the measure of poverty that a man wants more than he has, of his ignorance that he wants so much that is not worth having. Detachment is only better in name, as the extreme of the ascetic life sounds better than the extreme of self-indulgence, whereas both are equally extremes.

The ideal is, of course, the Higher Third of this new pair of opposites, non-attachment, which Hui-neng calls the 'fundamental principle' of the Dharma or manifested Truth. In Eckhart's tremendous words, 'Perfect detachment is without regard. It has no mind to be below nor yet above; it is minded to be master of itself, loving none and hating none. The only thing it desires is to be one and the same, for to be either this or that is to want something. He who is this or that is somebody, but detachment wants altogether nothing. It leaves all things unmolested.'[1]

What should we do about desire and attachment in our efforts to reach that pure detachment which is non-attachment? Crush it, say some. 'Kill out desire; but if thou killest it take heed lest from the dead it should again arise.' Sublimate it, say psychologists, leading it from lower to higher ends. 'The wise man will give up a lesser pleasure to obtain a greater joy.' 'Blend them and use them' says Huang Po. 'Do not build up your views on your senses and thoughts, but at the same time do not seek the

[1] Quoted in Dr Suzuki's *Mysticism, Christian and Buddhist*, p. 14.

Mind away from your senses and thoughts. When you are neither attached to nor detached from them, you enjoy unobstructed freedom; you have your seat of enlightenment.' Of the two ends of the elastic cord which binds us to the object of desire we must learn to drop that end which is in the mind. Only then can we enjoy the object in all innocence. For in all consideration of the problem of self and circumstance the factor of mind is paramount. That which created the circumstance must dominate the relationship. There is a Chinese story of two monks who argued about a pennant blown in the wind. 'It is the flag which moves', said one. 'It is the wind which moves', said the other. So they asked the Master to decide. 'It is neither', said the Master, 'it is the mind that moves.' This relationship between the outer and inner forms of reality is extremely intimate. We in the West, say the Chinese and Japanese, boast of our dominion over nature, of the conquest of this and that. In the East, nature and man are partners, fellow workers to a common end. It is wise to 'help nature and work on with her; and nature will regard thee as one of her creators and make obeisance'.[1] As Li Po, China's greatest poet remarked, 'We never grow tired of each other, the mountain and I.'

Conscious co-operation between subject and object, the former aware of the constant changes visible in both, will remove a host of the present worries which are parent to our suffering. The sense of flow will come more easily, conflict be reduced, and the practice of projection will be slowly replaced by its opposite, which psychologists call introjection. For there cannot be true relationship unless the subject is aware that much of the object is not merely his own creation, in the sense that his past deeds made it so, but has no existence other than as a picture of his own imagining flung on the screen of circumstance. We complain of all things save our insufficiency, and really believe that we do what we do because of the weather, our ailments, the Government, or the machinations, already referred to, of 'they'. The task of introjection is difficult, for room must be made in the mind for all our deficiencies, from lack of concentration to lack of understanding, which at present we hand on to someone or something else. Thus we are 'hurt'

[1] *The Voice of the Silence.*

by a host of happenings—or so we say. In truth the happenings happen; we choose to react by being hurt, that is, by feeling the injury in our pride or self-esteem. Yet no one hurts us; 'If any man be unhappy', said Epictetus, 'let him know that it is by reason of himself alone.'

If we are not to hurt ourselves by our reactions, we must learn to cease to react, until such time as the neurotic 'feelings' or claims of self have died. 'Our mind', said Hui-neng, 'should stand aloof from circumstance, and on no account should we allow them to influence the function of our mind.' In Western parlance, 'things sent to try us' are too often allowed to succeed.

But to concentrate too much on the subject will be to fall from the Middle Way. My present muddled view on the interrelation of me and circumstance will remain in a muddle until I can rise in consciousness and view the relationship from a Higher Third. 'Common people', said Hui-neng over a thousand years ago, 'attach themselves to objects without; and within they fall into the wrong idea of the Void. When they can free themselves from attachment to objects when in contact with objects, and free themselves from fallacious views on the doctrine of the Void, they will be free from delusions within and illusions without.'

For in the end, if our metaphysical premises are true, all that we know within and without is untrue, a fallacy of seeming wherein nothing is. We can but adjust our changing selves to the changing substance of our self-wrought circumstance, and in our 'walking on' take the whole of it, ourselves included, forward on the Way. From this improved, if not exalted point of view we begin to see our lives and our surroundings not only as sufficient for our needs, but 'right'. All of it is for us the 'right' experience. There is no greater teacher than daily life; everything can teach us something, and if we are bored with it, or feel frustrated in its grip, the fault is within us and not in the circumstance. 'The fault, dear Brutus, is not in our stars but in ourselves that we are underlings', and if we wish to be lordlings, let us arise and remould, first, ourselves and only much later, if at all, the world about us.

The use and abuse of possessions

All this must change our views about possessions. Possessions of what? Of the Self, or self? We take nothing with us to the state of consciousness between two lives save character, not even our neighbours' esteem or loathing, which was their reaction to us as part of their environment. Do we, then, own anything? Are we not trustees of all that we possess, to use for the common weal? Certainly this applies to ancient things of beauty, which others loved before us, and others again will love in the days to come. Even perishable things should surely not be wasted; there is no excuse for waste of anything. We are managers rather than owners of our property, and if we do not want an article, there is someone else who does; let that person be found. We are all of us rich in relation to some poorer person, and if we hoard what others need we are worse than the dog in the manger; for the talent that we do not use goes bad, as food too long in a cupboard, and men grow ill for the wealth they have wasted or never used. We need for our adventuring toward right action some measure of Wabi,[1] that poverty of desire which is content, in thought if not in circumstance, with a little hut and the minimum of the body's needs. This is 'right' poverty, and cognate with right giving, for why should we keep what is nothing to us but responsibility? It needs a strong man to use his possessions wisely, and great is the man who can do it. For he knows 'the strength of no desire', and the fruits which are born of it. In a wealth of circumstance he is master of it, content to use it or to let it go. The Stoics applied these principles, and Epictetus leads the way. 'It is hard to combine the qualities of the carefulness of one who is affected by circumstance and the intrepidity of one who heeds them not. But it is not impossible; else were happiness impossible.' What, then, should we do? We should act as we do, he says, when we go to sea. 'I choose the master, the crew, the day, the opportunity. Then comes a sudden storm. What matters it to me? My part is fully done. The ship is foundering. What then have I to do? I do the only thing that remains to me—to be drowned without fear, without a cry, without upbraiding God, but knowing that what has been born must likewise perish. For

[1] See Suzuki's *Zen Buddhism and its Influence on Japanese Culture.*

I am not Eternity, but a human being, a part of the whole as an hour is part of the day. I must come like the hour and like the hour must pass.' What a man!

Thoreau, then, was right when he said, 'I know that the enterprise is worthy. I know that things work well. I have heard no bad news.'

Chapter 5

The Middle Way

*There is a Middle Way, O Bhikkhus, discovered
by the Tathagata, a path which opens the eyes
and bestows understanding, which leads to peace
of mind, to the higher wisdom, to full enlightenment, to Nirvana . . .*

DHAMMA-CAKKA-PPAVATTANA-SUTTA

THIS 'doctrine of the Mean', avoiding all extremes of every
kind, eschewing dogmatism, fanaticism and all intolerance, was
described in the first recorded sermon of the Buddha, and is one
of the basic principles of Buddhism. Here we are only concerned
with it as an ingredient in Right Action, for no act is ideally
right that swerves by a hair's breadth from the middle way
between all the pairs of opposites which collectively portray the
indivisible unity of the One, and still more falsely the Non-
duality which lies beyond One and Two.

First we must face it, the dual fact that the right way lies
between all extremes and that a million pairs of the opposites
divide our interest every moment of the waking day. The
duality is inevitable, and inherent in the manifestation in the
universe of THAT. It is therefore useless to proclaim in any
argument, 'There is no difference. It's all the same thing,
really.' True, the opposites are as the two sides of a coin,
complementary, but the two sides of a coin are different, as are
male and female, night and day. Some tension between the
opposites is equally inevitable. This twin polarity of the mag-
netic field, the positive and negative terminals of that form of
life we call electricity, the desire of the male and female for
each other, these create tension which will never die until the
two become one in a higher state in which both, though separate,

are merged in a higher unity. In the same way, in-breathing and out-breathing, work and rest are alternating states, and the presence of the one implies the existence, earlier or later in the illusion of time, of the other.

The 'Higher Third'

Meanwhile the human mind, dimly but deeply aware of its oneness with All-Mind, forever seeks for union. It will not find it in either opposite, nor in both, and still less in attempt at compromise. God and Mammon are truly alternates, and it has been interestingly said that compromise is the Devil. Right can never be a mixture of right and wrong, and at any one moment we either create or destroy. The solution of the problem, the integration of the pairs, the release from the tension, is to be found in what I have elsewhere called a Higher Third, a point which makes a triangle with any pair, yet is not between them on their plane. As Jung pointed out in *The Secret of the Golden Flower*, no problem is ever solved on its own plane. Only when consciousness is raised to a higher level does the tension fade, and the problem, being seen in a new light, is no longer a problem. The faculty by which the opposites are finally transcended is the intuition, the instrument in man for the awareness of Prajna, the supreme Wisdom which, with supreme Compassion is one of the ultimate two. 'The Prajna-eye', says Dr Suzuki, 'placing itself on the boundary-line of Oneness and Manyness . . . of Enlightenment and Ignorance, takes in these two worlds at a glance as one Reality. Prajna is not on this side, nor on that side nor in the middle; when it is subjected to discrimination it is lost, it is no more there.'[1]

In his *Supreme Doctrine*, Benoit calls this Higher Third the Superior Principle which reconciles the two inferior principles, and he adds a further point of importance. Man, he says, is apt to see only the antagonistic character of the Two Dragons, not their complementary aspect. He sees them in combat, but he does not see them collaborating in this struggle. Yet the pairs are truly in collaboration to produce that which transcends them, and they can only die as duality in the arms of that which gave them birth.

[1] *Essays in Zen Buddhism*, Third Series, p. 256.

There is a Buddhist scripture immensely popular in China and Japan which is variously translated, for the Chinese ideographs are highly compressed in meaning. In Dr Suzuki's translation we read,

'Pursue not the outer entanglements,
Dwell not in the inner void;
When the mind rests serene in the oneness of things,
The dualism vanishes by itself.'

In this serenity of mind or heart (*hsin* can mean either and much more), the pairs coalesce.

To set up what you like against what you dislike,
This is the disease of the mind:
When the deep meaning (of the Way) is not understood
Peace of mind is disturbed and nothing is gained.

But,

When dualism no more obtains
Even oneness itself remains not as such.

The joy of flow

One way to achieve this peace of mind is to let go of either bank of the river and to be content, and it is a deep content, to flow with the stream. So long as a man walks on, or flows, or perceives his substance to exist of motion alone as modern scientists are bold enough to declare, much will happen. All flows; to stop is illusion, and to stop on either bank of the river of flow is a cause of pain. The man who keeps moving, not in aggressive action but in full serenity of mind, has nothing to fear from any thing in the world. He is impregnable, for he has no possessions to lose, no goal to attain. He has no feelings where he has no self to be hurt; balanced, he cannot fall, and he sees the field of action in its entirety. Thus he is one with that 'Power divine which moves to Good', the principle of Enlightenment which dwells in everything, and he knows, beyond all reasoning, that all is as it should be, that things indeed work well. If this is a hard saying it will seem less hard at a later stage of the journey.

But the Middle Way is a knife edge, to achieve and to maintain. 'A tenth of an inch's difference, and heaven and earth are set apart.' It moves between all extremes, 'between the carelessness of the average sensual man and the strained overeagerness of the zealot for salvation. To achieve it one must walk delicately, and to maintain it, must learn to combine the most intense alertness with a tranquil and self-denying passivity, the most indomitable determination with a perfect submission to the leadings of the spirit.'[1] Yet even the knife edge must not be sought too strenuously, for such effort may be born of self.

The thousand pairs of opposites might be graded from obvious to subtle, from easy to synthesize to all but impossible, and maybe this analysis has been done. They could be tabulated from the physical plane to the highest realms of thought, or from lying wide on each side of the line to a nearness which, though wider than a hair's breadth, scarce divides the pair. Here we need but consider a few of particular value to our present exercise.

Theravada and Mahayana

The two main schools of Buddhism, the Theravada and Mahayana have been described by a hundred scholars. For myself I believe their seeming differences are complementary, a restoration of a longed-for balance in the human mind. The Theravada or older school drove deep into the mind of the individual; the later school drove out into the farthest corners of manifestation, losing in intensity what it gained extensively. Comparison with the introvert and extrovert is obvious, and the Wisdom sought by one is equated with the Compassion practised by the other. These views explain their relative ideals, the Arhat and the Bodhisattva, between whom there is only relative emphasis. The Arhat is concerned with developing himself; the Bodhisattva with the salvation of mankind. Are these not relative and complementary aims? Can any man achieve perfection who leaves from the ambit of his thought the rest of the whole of which he is an infinitesimal part? Can any man be of genuine service to his fellow men who has not slain the self within and thus become one with life in all its forms?

In the world of science, that god which looms so largely in the Western firmament, the polarity of electrical forces, in

[1] Aldous Huxley: *The Perennial Philosophy*, p. 86.

which the positive and negative partition the field of their relationship, and move in tension to their mutual death and ever new beginning, is something that we use throughout the day. In the human body we need alternative work and rest, action and passivity. In the emotions we see how the hands that reach to cling or press away display the like and dislike in which so much of our energy is spent; between 'head' and 'heart' is ever a working though untrue duality. In the mind, the sceptic and dogmatic, the optimist and the pessimist go hand in hand; in temperament the Cavalier and the Roundhead fight within the self-same mind. But the fiercest tension is that between inner and outer, between the rational world of concrete things and values, and the irrational, inner life of generalized conceptions, unformed feelings and the power of the unconscious. Both are equally true and untrue, both of equal power, and they demand alike that man shall obey them. Yet both realities are incomparable and irreconcilable on the same level, for they belong to different degrees of the human order. We must therefore find the middle way on which to unite them, perhaps in that 'Self' which Jung describes as being born where the conscious and unconscious meet. Its growth is the process of individuation, as it is nowadays called, which is at least a long step on the road to Enlightenment.

In the daily life of the would-be spiritual man the Middle Way is that described by the Buddha himself in his first Sermon. 'There are two extremes, O Bhikkhus, which the man who has given up the world ought not to follow, the habitual practice on the one hand of those things depending on the passions, a low, unworthy way, unprofitable, fit only for the worldly-minded, and the habitual practice on the other hand of self-mortification, which is also painful, unworthy and unprofitable. There is a Middle Path, avoiding these two extremes. . . .' It is the Path which equally avoids all others, and will be considered later.

Inwardly the conflict of the opposites grows more subtle. Past and future are seen as a pair with this in common, that they are not direct experience. Of the one we have but the concepts of memory; of the other, the projection of present concepts into a belief of what may be. Yet a man is too often held by either or both. How many lean backwards into the past, or even turn and habitually face it; how many live in a future which may never come, thus robbing of useful thought and needed energy the eternal and the only fruitful Now?

Tariki and Jiriki

More subtle is the mind-produced division into Yes and No. The famous Buddhist school of the Madhyamikas, founded by Nagarjuna, was based on the Middle Way between affirmation and denial, between saying of any thing either yes or no. To say that all things exist is one point of view; the converse is to say that nothing exists. Neither is true, nor both of them. Sooner or later we must realize that no single thing is more than a rapidly changing bundle of characteristics, a form of motion as some scientists would say, but likewise we must, in the words of Eckhart, 'be free from *not*'. But these are matters of philosophy. Touching us more nearly is the distinction between Tariki and Jiriki, to use the Japanese terms. Jiriki is to obey the Buddha's injunction, 'Work out your own salvation, with diligence'; Tariki is to abandon self and finally to fling oneself into the arms of some Other Power which is universal. The ultimate synthesis of these is obvious even to the intellect, for whatever the efforts of the Self, which is changing, imperfect and partial, in the end the part must surrender to the Whole. Indeed the first flash of Satori, of Absolute awareness in the relative, only comes when personal effort fails in utter exhaustion, and as in Francis Thompson's 'Hound of Heaven', the pursued, at bay, finds that he is one with the Pursuer. But for those, and they are many, who find in our English poets the wisdom that their pen-companions in mere prose have failed to achieve, I beg of you to read again the poem 'If', by Rudyard Kipling, and flavour to the full its depth and subtlety.

The road climbs higher in its spiral progress up the hill. The wings of the two extremes grow closer, the distinctions between left and right, between right and wrong more narrow and ill-defined. The sense of flow grows stronger as the hand-holds on either bank are bravely abandoned. 'Individual consciousness', says Charlotte Woods,[1] 'is the adaptation to

[1] *The Self and its Problems*, p. 63.

specific purposes, by the body as an organ of action, of the flow of the universal consciousness.' As the centre of individuation in the individual, so to speak, shifts from self to Self, and thence to a Self more conscious of its own unreality, the Path grows narrower still, and the first glimpse is attained of the Emptiness which alone contains it. Sunyata, emptiness, void alike of things and no things, is 'the non-difference between yes and no, and the truth escapes us when we say "it is" and when we say "it is not"'. It lies in the Zen koan *mu*,[1] the ultimate 'not' which is not yes and not not, in a world where A is A and also not-A, on the plane of the reciprocal identification of the opposites. If this is at the moment the vaguest of concepts, it is well even now to see that it exists, for at least it will rob the inward tension of some validity to know that the battlefield of this versus that is a product of our false imagining. For here, on the actual razor's edge, *all* statements are invalid, and every word is wrong; and much of the vast field of noble thought, in the scriptures of Mahayana Buddhism, is dedicated to making this one thought plain. 'The Tao that can be expressed is not the eternal Tao', says the *Tao Tê Ching*, and logic cannot describe the Void. All statements couched in the potted concepts of words must err on one side or the other. Of every statement made the converse is also 'true'. Does this help when we next wish to be dogmatic, or intolerant of what we understand from another set of words from another unillumined mind?

The path grows narrower, more strait in the Biblical sense, and few there be that find it. For there is less and less of the one who treads it, less of a goal to be reached or motive for reaching it. Just every thing is wrong because imperfect, every view but partial, and all our actions seem to be on one side or the other of the non-existent middle of the Middle Way!

Meanwhile we exist and seek that middle, and we must seek and find it partially in the world around, partially in the world within and only wholly when this pair has been transcended on the bridge which joins them. Let us then, 'draw a line from North to South, and see that there is neither East nor West'. Let us begin to coalesce the subject and object of our experience, the mind and the world it has made for us.

[1] Edward Conze: *Buddhism*, p. 136.

Chapter 6

Duties, Rights and Responsibilities

The Man who does not go through his appointed task in life has lived in vain.

THE VOICE OF THE SILENCE

It is better to do one's own duty than to perform another's well. There is danger in another's duty.

BHAGAVAD GITA

W H A T are my duties, rights and responsibilities in relation to things about me? The answer depends on the definition of 'my'. The self is clamorous for its rights, seeks to avoid its duties, and ignores its responsibilities. The Self admits its duties, is modest about its rights and exact in its assumption of responsibilities. In the ideal, of course, these three should be smoothly integrated in a delicate sense of reciprocity with nature, neighbours and the field of circumstance.

The universe seems built on a hierarchy, whatever the politicians may from time to time proclaim. Men are not born equal, whatever Presidents may say; indeed, one of the most outstanding facts about them is that they are born astonishingly unequal, an argument in favour of the doctrine of rebirth. Whether the hierarchy be headed by God, a Guru, or a King, the principle is the same, and the feudal state, which is built on an intricate relation of rights and duties, has much to commend it. For we are all of us deeply indebted to our fellow men of all degree, individually and collectively, and we must learn to receive with gratitude and to give with a measure that joyously overflows. We are all trustees of the common wealth, a platitude so mouthed by politicians that it is easy to forget that it is true; meanwhile we owe and are owed a vast variety of commodity, from money and goods to thought and kindliness. For such as we give we acquire merit, credit in terms of character, as the Buddhists say. And this is reasonable. If it is true, as written in the *Dhammapada*, that 'all we are is the result of what we have thought; it is founded on our thoughts, made up of our thoughts', then the good we do comes back to us, for as we think so we become, and we are what we have made ourselves, by actions 'good' or 'bad'. We therefore acquire merit by right actions, and demerit, and consequent suffering, by all that we do which is wrong. True, one day we shall have no motive, even for the best of our actions, and there will be left no self to receive the benefits of good, but we are not yet at this height on the slopes of Everest.

The Sharing of Merit

If all life is one life, and men are truly brothers even as the fingers of one hand, then all that we do affects all others, and indeed the whole universe, and our good deeds and evil deeds have influence on the smallest thing that lives. It is therefore not only possible but unavoidable that our merit shall be shared with others, and the deliberate sharing of merit, or transfer to all that suffer within that 'mighty sea of sorrow formed of the tears of men', is practical, and is happening every day. The famous 18th Vow of Amida Buddha which is the basis of Pure Land Buddhism, never to enter Nirvana until all beings shall have arrived in the Heaven of his own Enlightenment, is poetic imagery for fact. Meanwhile we must achieve such accumulation of merit as will enable us to save or to begin to save mankind from the follies of its contented ignorance.

When the merit is acquired it is no sacrifice to surrender it. To sacrifice is to make holy, in that the thing or act of merit is offered by self to the Not-self, by the part to the service of the whole. This is why the greater shall always be sacrificed to the less, age to youth, the teacher to the taught, wisdom to those that need it. From this point of view 'there is no such thing as sacrifice. There is opportunity to serve, and he who overlooks it robs himself.'[1] Service, therefore, to the Self, the best within us, should be natural, not an effort, though here as ever there is

[1] Talbot Mundy: *Om*, p. 329.

the wrong way and the right. Wrong sacrifice may be ill-concealed selfishness, and sacrifice that is not duty, in the highest sense attainable, may be definitely wrong, as well as most tiresome for one's neighbours. As I put it in *Walk On!*, 'Service out of a strained sense of duty is an insult to the person or community served, for it lacks the very basis of service, a recognition that life is one.'[1]

Yet service may be selfish, for it is in itself a process for removing self, and we are much the better for the loss of what we give, whether of money, goods, or time and thought and kindliness expended on another's need. Meanwhile we serve. By example, for there is no greater gift to another than 'the spectacle of achieved holiness'. This is the gift of the monk or Buddhist Bhikkhu to mankind, a living proof that the pleasures of the world are well exchanged for the holy life, and that by being 'abstemious in the satisfaction of desire' we gain more than we lose. Lower than visible progress on the Way is teaching about it; the Guru great and small is ever of service to mankind. Lower still yet necessary, and never to be despised, is the worker who, content with the physical plane, does well what someone must, for love or money, do, and does it happily. The story of Martha and Mary has always puzzled me.[2] The two sisters sat at the feet of the Master, but Mary left it to her sister to do the physical work of ministering to his needs, and continued to do, what? To express her devotion, or to learn his teaching, or both? Eckhart (I use Evans' translation) is most helpful. He is speaking of the danger of being so caught up in higher experiences that one is unwilling to return to the earthly job in hand. How about the outward works, he asks, 'works of charity, such as teaching and comforting those in need. Are we debarred from these?' And he answers, of the two ways, 'the one is perfect, the other very profitable. Mary was praised for choosing the best, and Martha's life was very useful, serving Christ and his disciples. . . . It is all the same thing. We have but to root ourselves in this ground of contemplation to make it fruitful in works, and the object of contemplation is achieved.' Elsewhere, however, he says that whatever the love expressed in Mary's

[1] p. 61.
[2] St Luke, Ch. 10, v. 38-42.

devotion 'we ought to get over amusing ourselves with such raptures for the sake of that better love, to accomplish through loving service what men most need, spiritually, socially or physically'. And he goes on, 'As I have often said, if a person were in such a rapturous state as St Paul once entered, and he knew of a sick man who wanted a cup of soup, it would be far better to withdraw from the rapture for love's sake and serve him who is in need.' And this is no remote comparison, for it is visible in the smallest group that works under a teacher. There are always those who hang on the least word of the Guru, regardless of the physical world, and those who arrange the chairs or fetch the tea and see that the holy one is at least comfortable. What then, was the 'one thing needful' which Mary possessed? I do not know.

But we cannot be Martha and Mary at the same time, nor can we at the same time serve God and Mammon. We can live a life which is a sad but at present necessary mixture, immersed in the world for most of the day but finding time for the meditation or the like which lifts the mind beyond its sway. But the will is bent on the journey up or down; to be released and free, or be bound contented with our discontent and only free to complain that we are not free. This is a choice that must be made and the choice is a grave one. Meanwhile we must render to Caesar the things that are Caesar's, of rates and taxes, of due conformity with our neighbour's code of morals, and obedience, while we are members, to the rules of our club. Within, we are or are becoming free of the rules which others have given us, whether of moral laws, the laws of parking motor cars, alike more honoured in the breach than in the observance, or the laws of our neighbour as to what is and what is not 'done'. But inward freedom does not give us licence to disobey. In the world of men we have our duty to perform.

The meaning of duty

Why do we loathe the word—or worship it? Surely we have a wrong grasp of its meaning to hate it so, or to make of it a merciless and loveless god. It has the connotation of compulsion,

---

[2] Suzuki: *Mysticism, Christian and Buddhist*, p. 14, quoting from Blakney's translation.

and compulsion implies the existence of Someone able to compel. But surely D. H. Lawrence was right in 'Work'.

> There is no point in work
> unless it absorbs you
> like an absorbing game.
>
> If it doesn't absorb you
> if it's never any fun
> don't do it.

How can we make our duty fun, to be neither slaves to it, nor abject in devotion? The word means what is due, what we owe to circumstance and our neighbour by reason of what we are, have done. Thus duty should be the reflection in man of the Dharma or basic plan of the universe, if we could find out what that is. It is the agenda for this life or this moment, what next 'ought', because it is owed, to be done. If we refuse to pay, the debit is carried forward, if need be to the next life; for there is no justice in the world, no harmony, if a debt can forever be left unpaid. 'The man who does not go through his appointed task in life has lived in vain.' Yet none appointed it. We have ourselves prepared our duty, and if we leave it undone it will wait for us; meanwhile another must do what we have refused to do, and gain the merit thereby for himself and all mankind.

The only right motive for duty done is the service of the Self within, that the Self, the more quickly purged of the consequence of error, may the more swiftly find Enlightenment. Here the *Bhagavad Gita* speaks for all mankind. Such a man 'hath no interest either in that which is done or that which is not done, and there is not in all things any object on which he may place dependence. Therefore perform thou that which thou hast to do, at all times unmindful of the event; for the man who doeth that which he hath to do, without attachment to the result, obtaineth the Supreme.'

'Unmindful of the event', that is the secret of right action, but how hard! For it implies not only indifference to the claims of self, that ever seeks praise for the least duty done, but it calls for a tolerance which is very difficult indeed. Right tolerance is to accept that there is more than one way to the

Truth, and it is the supreme virtue of Buddhism. But it calls for a hair-breadth Middle Way. There is danger in another's duty, as the *Bhagavad Gita* again and again declares, yet the converse is as true, 'inaction in a deed of mercy is action in a deadly sin'. We should mind our own business, and allow our neighbour to attempt to obey the Buddha's last command, 'Work out your own salvation with diligence.' But it is a difficult feat of tolerance to allow our neighbour to be right; and more difficult still to allow him to be wrong and to sow the seeds which must lead to a life of sorrow. Yet few can learn from another's error, still less from another's words, when desire is pulling strongly in a self still vigorous. *The Voice of the Silence* speaks of the Arhat's 'helpless pity for the men of karmic sorrow; the fruit of karma Sages dare not still'. To see, as the wiser man can see, the ungarnered sorrow of a course of action, and yet to lift no finger to prevent the lesson being learnt is bitterness indeed, yet the child must learn to walk by falling, and as Dostoevsky said, 'To go wrong in one's own way is better than to go right in someone else's.'

Duty, then, is what is due to be done, and it should be done without regard to pleasure or pain, but because it is due to be done. This is a major difficulty, to withhold from the job in hand the emotional factor of like/dislike. We cannot like the whole of our duty all the time, but we can abstract from it the habit of desire and its reverse, repulsion. If we can learn to do the next thing to be done for no other reason than because it *is* the next thing to be done, we shall have less cause for putting it off, or for putting it onto the shoulders of someone who is in no way bound to do it. As we shall see, there is a technique for this habit as for all else we should do, and the secret lies in the mind. As such it is better considered later.

But whether we like or dislike the next thing on our personal agenda, it is a debt to be paid to circumstance, and like all debts it is best paid at the moment it falls due. If we have trust in the law which seems to govern the universe, then all that happens happens rightly in the sense at least of the right time and place. If nature presents a bill is there a better time for its payment, or a better place, than here and now? Like washing up, it is better to do it while the dishes and the occasion are still warm.

'Pay as you Go'

I have developed this in the thesis of 'Pay as you Go'. Each act disturbs the pendulum of nature, affects its harmony, as a stone thrown into a pool. A debt is incurred, to restore the harmony, and its payment is duty, for the debt is due. The deed may be complex, involving the three planes of the physical, emotional and mental; the balance must be restored on each of them—and so it will if the law of Karma, cause/effect, be true. But is the debt paid as a man takes coins from his pocket to pay for a meal, or will he be haled to prison as a debtor in six months' time? It is for the debtor to say. We get nothing for nothing in this life; we pay for everything, in money, time, interest or some other giving of the life within us. Is it not therefore wise to pay swiftly, generously, for thus the account with heaven will be neither in credit nor debit, but once more balanced, as all accounts should be?

It is surely wise to pay generously, for thus duty spills over into Dana, charity, and the self is given away with what is paid. What is left is so much more emptiness, the Void which alone is full, even as a room from which years of unwanted, useless goods are taken away has more space for the sun and air. If we are given injury, insult and complaint, we are hurt; but it is self that feels the injury, and self has no right to be there. Should we give to the thief? Jesus so advised, and Epictetus pointed out that the thief is the greater loser by the theft. For the old man loses but his cloak; the thief, his honour. You would speak of his deserts, and of our duty to see that a thief is given them? How many wise men have advised that were we to get our deserts we should do poorly? Is it not better to give and give, that with the time and money and energy we give to those who need it something of the self that hinders us from giving may be given away too? The payment may be made in many ways; in visible things, of goods and money; in time, and the busiest man has most of it to give; in interest in another's problems; in gratitude, not for the worth of the gift but for the thought which gave it. Should we lend, in the face of Polonius' advice to Laertes? Perhaps not, for truly 'loan oft loseth both itself and friend, and borrowing dulls the edge of husbandry'. It is better to give; if the debt is repaid it is the more pleasant to receive it when it had been forgotten. More valuable still is under-standing, for surely this is the deepest debt that we owe to our brother men.

In the ending of any relationship, is it not better to be deeply generous, that the link may be truly dissolved and no longer a fetter on the way? Whether in business, divorce or the sharing of a garden roller, it is better to give as the Buddhist gives of love, compassion, joy and equanimity. 'And he lets his mind pervade the whole world, above, below, around and everywhere with heart of love, far-reaching and beyond measure. . . .' Thus have the great ones of the earth ever acted, and the habit puts an end to duty as a boring, dreary, dull thing to be done.

So much for 'Pay as you Go', offered as the fruit of experi-ence. As a method of handling duty it works.

A lesson learnt is an account closed; duty done leaves the doer the better for the deed. For until all karmic accounts are closed there must be a self to settle them—one way or the other. For good done with an eye to profit, of merit on earth or in heaven, needs the return of the self to receive the reward. And this is a further advantage of Pay as you Go, that the habit of payment becomes so formed that the self is more and more left out of the reckoning. Good is done for its own sake—'And because right is right, to follow right were wisdom in the scorn of consequence.'[1]

Then what of rights? If the above is true we have none, or so few that it is a waste of time demanding them. For they can but belong to the self, and the self must rise to demand them. Where another's are invaded, however, it may be right to defend them, for we are warriors, as already quoted, in that we fight against injustice and evil in all its forms. But this is the field of right action; we are trying to remain in the field of right acting, in the sense of the principles of action to whatever end applied.

Responsibility and irresponsibility

Then what of responsibility? And its converse, equally im-portant, irresponsibility? I have long been fascinated by the Middle Way between these two. On the one hand is the com-

[1] Tennyson: *Oenone*.

plex of thought revolving about duty, which Marcus Aurelius calls the 'ambit of our moral purpose'; and on the other, the divine inconsequence of the *Tao Tê Ching*, the 'purposelessness' which is left when the highest purpose has died.

I find them compatible, for I have that type of mind in which irreconcilables may lodge together happily. In the world of men I believe in the strict allocation and performance of responsibility. Either I am responsible or I am not. In the first case I accept the responsibility, and though in turn I may make others sub-responsible to me, remain responsible to those above me and shield subordinates accordingly. This is the tradition of all hierarchies, from an office to an army, and it is clearly 'right'. In the same way, if I am not responsible, I refuse to be either praised or blamed for a matter with which I am not concerned. But knowing that all appearance is an illusion (as even science, that bastard with a noble name, can prove), a fleeting glimpse of a cross-section in time of a continuous process of becoming, I refuse to take responsibility any more seriously than I take the 'I' supposed to assume it. If I am so immensely unimportant, how can it be so important what I do? But here the relations with others, involved in all consideration of duty, must be taken in. For in the world of men, a relative world of relationships, responsibility is inseparable from the allied concepts of duty, honour and good faith. Hence the importance of the correct assumption and performance of it. Only in the deeper recesses of the mind, where the 'I' has its roots in a more universal Self, can the doctrine of irresponsibility be entertained. The self has purpose, personal ambition. The deeper Self, which views the cycle of life and death from a point nearer the unmoving centre of the wheel, has less purpose, less ambition, and is closer to the joyous purposelessness of the waterfall, the sunset and the rose. For ultimately there can be only one purpose in the Universe, its own, and he is a fool who attempts to define it.

In the daily round, the process of cause/effect which the East calls Karma provides a chart or index to one's position, and would enable one to find at any moment the net resultant of past causes, if only one could know all the causes which have led to that effect. One cannot, yet it is from this resultant and from this alone that duty springs, whether the source be no more than a vague impulse to pursue this course of action rather than that, or a reasoned analysis of all the calls upon one's will and time.

If some, regarding the whole field of duty created by their own past karma, choose some particular portion of the field in which to operate in that life, or month or day, they assume such a work as duty, and it thereby becomes their duty. If part of this duty involves the assumption of responsibility for some act, then this responsibility becomes itself a duty, and enters the Stoic Emperor's 'ambit of one's moral purpose'. Strictly speaking all else, not being one's duty, is waste of time, and therefore of opportunity for useful experience, but most of us like time off, even from doing what we know we ought to do because we have agreed, if only with ourselves, to do it.

Then, just as we are struggling manfully with duty, pitting will against desire, and strength of purpose against the demands of the flesh, the voice of Tao is heard. And the voice of Tao is no cool, angelic admonition but a great roar of laughter, of good fat belly laughter, and the warrior in the cause of duty pauses and gets pink. Then he begins to argue, and Tao, which is one of the names of life and was therefore old before man was born, laughs louder still. For the Tao admits no bondage, and duty therein is a word unknown. Do the winds assume responsibility as they sweep the sky? They blow. Do rivers flow beneath the urge of duty? They flow. So does the Taoist, upon the river of life, without compulsion, without argument or aim. He is divinely irresponsible, doing what ought to be done because he does what he is. He acts in accordance with his being, without thought, without feeling. He manifests himself, and ever a deeper part of himself, according as he lets all minor purpose flow upon the winds.

And the truth? Between, of course, as always. Like a woman when asked to choose between two presents, the answer is both, a keen responsibility in action with a mind kept un-attached, irresponsible, without producing cause/effect, and therefore free.

Chapter 7

Action and Inaction

Both action and inaction may find room in thee;
thy body agitated, thy mind tranquil, thy Soul
as limpid as a mountain lake.

THE VOICE OF THE SILENCE

ACTION and inaction are yet another of the Pairs of Opposites, and their 'higher third' is of course Non-action. As between the two the relation is a matter of emphasis, for no man is ever totally in action, and there is no such thing in manifestation as complete inaction. In a recent lecture Lord Samuel spoke of energy as existing 'in two states, active and quiescent, which passed easily from one to the other'. The conception of quiescent energy was 'a necessary inference from observed phenomena'. The same might be said for dynamic watchfulness. Nor is either of the extremes preferable in itself. There is no virtue in inaction, for action need not bind the actor. It is not action which binds but action born of ignorance, the false belief that we are separate individuals with separate interests, and that action for the benefit of the part alone can benefit the individual. These are the 'knots of the heart' which only the study of right action and inaction will slowly dissolve.

The word action is easy to understand, but the opposite, and the 'higher third' collating them, are variously described as inaction and non-action. In the use of references these two must not be confused. First, then, let us clarify the distinction between action and its opposite, rest. We act on three planes at least, physical, emotional and mental. The action may be expressed or unexpressed, visible or invisible, conscious or at best subconscious. The body may be still but is only partly at rest, for the autonomic nervous system is still functioning, and processes of many kinds, from breathing, the heart-beat and digestion to the complex rhythm of the building and destruction of the cells, go on unceasingly. Emotion may be quiescent, but the basic attitude to life, aggressive or receptive, friendly or resentful, animates the air with its particular wave-length, and no man's emotions are ever entirely at rest. The same applies to the mind. It is impossible to think of nothing, as those who first approach the practice of meditation glibly use this term. Mind-training enables the student to choose and maintain the object of thought, and at a later stage to pass in consciousness beyond the function of thought. For these only is it true to speak of 'the sleep of the mind my sword'; for most of us the machine of thought is at least 'ticking over' even when not deliberately used. But rest, however incomplete, is an alternative to work, and the rhythm is natural in large affairs and small. As the night after day so, in the ancient teaching, comes a period of rest between lives, when the complex, changing mind or character —we must not call it soul—digests a life's experience before returning to school for more lessons and more experience. Relaxation is a term allied to rest but not synonymous. All schools of work, whether of ballet or meditation, alike teach relaxation as a deliberate exercise, in order that the divers parts of the machine of self may be truly rested. It is because we have never trained ourselves in this difficult exercise that we need our holidays, the secret of which is change and hence relaxation of tension in the usual field of exercise. The cat is the visible example of physical relaxation, but Chuang-Tzu's analogy of the drunken man falling from a cart is entirely relevant. He is not hurt 'for he meets his accident in a different way. . . . Ideas of life, death, fear and the like cannot penetrate his breast, and so he does not suffer from contact with objective existence. If such security is to be got from wine, how much more is to be got from Tao?'

Acceptance and Passivity

On a higher plane are the concepts of acceptance and passivity. The former is central to the whole field of right acting, for unless the situation in its totality and all its parts are utterly accepted for what they are and in terms of their common 'suchness', there can be no right attitude towards them nor inaction in respect of them. To produce this acceptance the Chinese, as no doubt others, have produced a complete technique which proved of the greatest interest to C. G. Jung. In his commentary on *The Secret of the Golden Flower* he studies the Taoist concept of Wu-wei, of which more later. He translates it for his own purposes as 'letting things happen', a spiritual habit taught by Meister Eckhart. He admits that the exercises suggested are extremely difficult to keep up, but the effect is to release what he calls the cramp in the conscious and to let things happen without interference from self on any plane. 'In this way a new attitude is created, which accepts the irrational and unbelievable simply because it is what is happening.'[1] It is still harder to see that what we have come to accept, good, bad or indifferent as we still label it, is in the eyes of eternity completely and totally 'right', and harder still to realize that it is not necessarily our duty to act at once in order to make it more as we would have it be. For to accept implies a self-control from interference, which is as difficult for some as it is hard for others to be up and doing where it is clearly their duty to act. The result is interesting, and Dr Jung gives the words of a patient to describe it. 'I always thought that when we accept things they overpower us in one way or another. Now this is not true at all, and it is only by accepting them that we can define an attitude towards them', that is, dissolve the sense of attachment to the unconscious whole and stand up as an individual, able and willing to work out his own salvation with diligence. If this acceptance implies the acceptance of much suffering, what of it? It has been said that if you learn to suffer you will learn not to suffer; in other words, the suffering, in the common sense of the term, is something we add to the experience which is, like all else, but the effect of causes for which we are responsible. Once the eyes are lifted from the fact of suffering to that 'fundamental all-rightness of the universe', as Aldous Huxley calls it, the effects of the causes remain, but though we still 'support' the experience, for that is the meaning of the word, we no longer suffer.

Passivity is a wider concept than acceptance, and indeed Dr

[1] *The Secret of the Golden Flower*, p. 91.

Suzuki, in his famous essay on 'Passivity in the Buddhist Life'[1] equates it with the mystical acceptance of some Power in the universe greater than ourselves which must 'take over' when the powers of the individual are found inadequate. The dominance of Self-Power (Jiriki) in Zen Buddhism can go, he says, too far, for when the intellect knows that it has reached its limitations it must surrender to the intuition, the power of which is universal. In this sense the mind becomes passive to the greater force, the self becomes obedient to the whole of which it is part. Of this link between passivity and compassion we can speak later; here it is enough to quote the great writer's summary. 'Passivity means breaking up the hard crust of egotism and melting itself in the infinity of the Dharmadhatu (Realm of Truth). This melting is felt psychologically as a mood of receptivity, and, theologically interpreted, as the feeling of absolute dependence which I have designated in this essay as passivity. With followers of Zen this is 'being wholly possessed by Prajna' . . . (p. 290). This lifting of consciousness to a point of non-recognition of the opposites save as the rhythm of the tides, is the 'passive awareness' described in L. C. Beckett's *Neti Neti*, the state of being passively active or actively passive as the psychological type prefers.

But whatever the relative meaning of these allied terms of acceptance and passivity, there is a sense of contentment with conditions which comes from withholding from circumstance the power to wound or even to affect us. 'We should stand aloof from circumstance, and on no account should we allow it to influence the function of our mind.' Thus the Patriarch Hui-neng, but it is difficult to allow oneself to be 'pushed around', and to learn that the man who is growing inwardly must 'become as nothing in the eyes of men'. Meanwhile we are told to be patient. I have always regarded patience as a most pernicious vice, for it is usually a feeble cloak for laziness. When, however, it is advice to wait on the rhythm of events, and to find the right time for the right action the advice is good. But first, before passing from inaction to action, must we interfere? In the East the tendency is to do too little; in the West, too much. Once more we must seek for the balance. As

[1] *Essays in Zen Buddhism*, Second Series.

is said in *The Voice of the Silence,* 'The man who does not go through his appointed task in life has lived in vain.' Yet a few pages earlier we read, 'Inaction in a deed of mercy becomes action in a deadly sin.'

Perhaps the most perfect blend of the alternating forces is visible in Judo, the Japanese science of defeating one's opponent by his own force. In this form of wrestling the mind must first be balanced evenly between aggression and defence. Relaxed yet tense, the body follows a mind whose muscles are equally trained by long development. Unconcerned with thoughts of victory or defeat, or indeed with any thoughts at all, the man of Judo waits for the attack and when it comes answers without thought but with the instantaneous and 'spontaneous' counter-act which throws his opponent with the very force with which he moved in to attack. Here one can actually see the weak overcome the strong and the soft overcome the hard, as proclaimed in the *Tao Tê Ching,* for when the mind is truly inactive its action comes with the strength of Tao—or Zen—or the power of the Universe. But we are moving into Non-action, and must for the time being return.

Timing

For how much time, and what does time matter? What is time, for we must know if we would wisely use it. It is an illusion, albeit convenient for our understanding of Now. We cannot, as already described, ever 'know' the past or future, and the present is so brief that it is not measurable in time. There is left the Now in terms of daily experience, a concentration on and deep contentment with the job in hand. This is a matter of consciousness, which moves with inconceivable rapidity, and where it is not there is no time. But the universal processes are rhythmic, as the seasons, birth and death and the tides. Within these cycles, vast and infinitesimally small, we move, and in them act. But just as we cannot mount the camel which has not yet come nor the camel that has gone, so there is a right time for all action, could we find it. To act too soon or too late presumably makes a noise in the cosmic silence as a gear that is shifted violently too soon or late with the clutch. But these are the actions under our control. Yet the actions which act us, so to speak, the true experiences, take place out of time, as we know quite well. In the greatest moments of our life we say that 'time stood still'. For they took place in the Now, in the timeless moment which is the 'Nothing Between' of past and future, of any two mortal facts. To revert to Judo, or the kindred art of Kendo, fencing, all the teaching is directed to striking without sense of time. Between the will and the blow, between defensive intent and action there can be no pause, no act in time. Thus we pass further from inaction into action. With what motive? Why? Presumably not for the love of action, nor for the sake of interference. Above all let it be not for the sake of self, for here is wrong action which bears effects for years and lives to come. Surely, all is wrong action which moves to the self's aggrandizement; all right, which moves to the One in which all sense of self is dead. But where there is an act there is an actor, imperfect in all his parts. He can but keep the Middle Way in this as all things to the best of his ability, knowing that he must fail and, in due course, reap the harvest of his failure. Says *The Voice of the Silence*, 'Both action and inaction may find room in thee; thy body agitated, thy mind tranquil, thy Soul as limpid as a mountain lake.' For the moment only the smallest acts can be so perfectly performed, with the Self untouched by the body's action, but a single act, be it a throw in Judo, picking up a dropped umbrella or a letter of thanks, is at least a beginning.

The effort used must be proportionate to the deed, a statement as easy to make as difficult to obey. Most of us either lack the horse-power of mind to do the major actions properly; the rest of us use twice the energy needed, and exhaust ourselves in cracking a nut. The secret is never to go entirely into action, but while harnessing will and thought and physical energy, to leave the Self, the mind at its highest, untouched by the event. As Chuang-Tzu wrote, 'Every one who attaches importance to the external becomes internally without resource.' In the perfect act there is a reaching out or down to effect the act determined; the inner man, the semi-enlightened man, draws back at will, the richer by the experience. And when we succeed just a little on this narrow way? 'Self-gratulation, O Disciple, is like unto a lofty tower, up which a haughty fool has climbed.

Thereon he sits in prideful solitude and unperceived by any but himself.'[1]

And so in time the student moves nearer to that central point where there is action in inaction, inaction in action. It is a matter of total awareness, looking both ways, outward to the field of action and inwards to the higher consciousness which, changing though it is, moves nearer to the Light. Aldous Huxley calls this total awareness 'a primary, choiceless, impartial response to the present situation as a whole',[2] and Lily Abegg talks of 'total thinking'[3] as the Eastern method of enveloping and in that way understanding an idea or situation. It is a nearer approach to the ideal condition of No-mind, and W. J. Gabb applies it in his well-known chapter on the 'Address to the Situation'.[4]

Dispassionate action

At the mid-point between action and inaction lies the complete dispassion which is the ideal of the few and the horror of the many. Most of us are so ruled by emotion, however hotly we deny the charge, that the expression of genuine dis-interest, or non-attachment to the act is regarded as cold and inhuman. Yet Goethe praised it. 'What attracted me in Spinoza', he wrote, 'was the boundless disinterestedness which shone forth from every sentence. That marvellous saying, 'Whoso loves God must not desire God to love him in return', with all the premisses on which it rests and the consequences that flow from it, permeated my whole thinking . . . so that the bold saying of mine, 'If I love thee, what is that to thee?' came strictly from my heart.'[5] The secret of such self-control is control of reaction. 'Wherever the eye looks, the heart is directed also', says C. G. Jung, in his examination of the movement of the Light. If the eye looks up the heart follows, and when the eye looks inward to Self, as the nearest yet achieved to the Light, the bonds to self and its interests weaken. But only he who has practised this divine austerity can begin to know 'The Strength of no Desire', which is the magnificent phrase by Dr Suzuki for the book of autographs I compiled while in Japan.

[1] *The Voice of the Silence.* [2] *Adonis and the Alphabet,* p. 69.
[3] *The Mind of East Asia.* [4] *The Goose is Out,* Ch. 8.
[5] Quoted in Warner Allen: *The Timeless Moment,* p. 212.

Wu-wei, or action in inaction

So we approach the field of Taoism, often described as the mother of Zen Buddhism, and its central concept, in itself a spiritual force as great as the universe, *wei-wu-wei*. In one way this is a process of undoing rather than doing, of undoing the knots tied up by the self in its false belief of permanence. But it is far more than 'doing nothing'. The phrase as usually quoted is Wu-wei, which means no act or non-action. But in full it is wei-wu-wei, which means action-no-action, which is very different. The first is one-sided, the other exquisitely balanced in the Nothing Between. It is action in inaction and inaction in action. It is the heart of the phrase, 'In the world, not of it.' It is action uninfluenced by the results of action, an act in which the actor is not involved. In the words of the *Bhagavad Gita*, 'One must learn what is action to be performed, what is not to be performed, and what is inaction. The path of action is obscure. That man who sees inaction in action and action in inaction is wise among men; he is a perfect performer of all action.' In the words of Master Lu Tzu, 'Non-action prevents a man becoming entangled in form and image. Action in inaction prevents a man from sinking to numbing emptiness and a dead nothingness.'[1] The secret is a perfect balance on the centre of the Middle Way. Greater than any action is the right letting things happen, when this itself becomes right action. As Dr Jung points out, our consciousness is always interfering in the growth of the mind, and refuses to allow the unconscious to wed the conscious in a greater unity. The self must learn not to interfere with the growth of the Self towards enlightenment. This in turn involves permission to act spontaneously, which is not in the least the same thing as acting impulsively, when the impulse comes from the self and not the Self. The source of such unplanned action must be the intuition; thought may rationalize the process later. To follow impulse blindly is the way of evil; the hunch or whim of the moment is unlikely to spring from a level higher than emotion which, unlit by Buddhi, is a dangerous guide. Nor, of course, is inaction, even alone, to be confused with the laziness and dull inertia which, though rationalized as non-interference, is the cause of most of our non-doing.

[1] *The Secret of the Golden Flower*, p. 59.

The Non-action of Tao

So we come to the *Tao Tê Ching*, the classic of Taoism and the mother of Zen. Like Zen, Tao has nothing to say, and 'the Tao that can be expressed is not the eternal Tao'. It is ever inactive and yet there is nothing that it does not do. 'When one looks at it one cannot see it; when one listens to it one cannot hear it. However, when one uses it it is inexhaustible.' When there is no self we can do anything. 'Man stands in his own shadow and wonders why it is dark.' In other words, get out of your own way! But the enigmatic phrases of the *Tao Tê Ching* are expanded by Chuang Tzu, the great mind which in the fourth century B.C. developed the Master's sayings and made of them a complete philosophy. Beyond action and inaction, he says, is Non-action. 'Rest in Inaction', he says (in the sense of my Non-action), 'and the world will be good of itself. Cast your slough. Spit forth intelligence. Ignore all differences. Become one with the infinite. Release your mind. Free your soul. Be vacuous. Be Nothing!' What a perfect man is this, so one with Absolute that he neither acts nor is actionless. 'For the perfect man employs his mind as a mirror. It grasps nothing; it refuses nothing. It receives but does not keep.' For him there is no need of charity or virtue and no duty to be done. 'Form and virtue and charity, these are the accidentals of the spiritual. Apprehending Tao he is in accord with virtue. He leaves charity and duty alone. He treats ceremonies and music as adventitious. And so his mind is at peace.' With his consciousness at home in the world of Prajna, the Wisdom beyond thought, he has no consciousness of virtue, for he flows with the flow of the universe, and all that he does is right. Being beyond the opposites of act and no-act, and all the others which man invents for his own blind purposes, he is not troubled by the conflicts and tensions of the man who has not Tao. Wanting nothing he gains all, and in action he is perfect, for 'he accomplishes everything without doing it'.

All this, however, is too high for us. For a while we must descend and face the central doctrine of Buddhism, and perhaps of all philosophy of daily life, the ultimate law of the universe, Karma, which may be partially translated as Cause/effect.

Chapter 8

Action and Reaction

This being, that becomes; from the arising of this,
that arises; this not becoming, that does not
become, from the ceasing of this, that ceases.

MAJJHIMA NIKAYA

Karma is a living law. Our deeds provide it
bodies, its hands to bless or to chastise. ANON

THE doctrine of Karma (Pali: Kamma) of Action/Reaction, is
central to this work, for with its overtones and undertones it can
provide the technique of right acting and hence of right action.
What can be more important? 'A man becomes what he does.
Can this doctrine be refuted? If it be true it is the most important
and the most neglected truth in the world.'[1] It is far older than
Buddhism, and the Indian sages knew it well. But the Buddha
gave new life to it and made it central, and we in the West must
understand it. 'The Occidental will never understand the teachings of the great sages of the Orient until he realizes in a
scientific sense the fundamental and far-reaching import of
Karma and rebirth when looked upon in the Oriental way,
as immutable laws governing the whole Cosmos.'[2] If true
it is neither of East nor West; if untrue it has waited long for
someone to refute it. The word has many meanings. Basically
it means action, with the connotation of action/reaction. It may
be used as the cause of results, but more often as the effect of
causes. Thus one speaks of the Karma of an act or line of action
as its consequences, and though these may be regarded as good
or bad the usual sense of the term is the unpleasant results of
wrong action. It is, however, as the law connecting action and

[1] Loftus Hare: *Mysticism of East and West*, pp. 213-4.
[2] Evans-Wentz: *Tibetan Yoga and Secret Doctrines*, p. 47.

reaction that it is best considered, for this raises it from the
dreary level of cosmic accountancy, almost amounting to
fatalism, wherein each act produces an effect of exactly the same
kind on the foolish doer.

A difficult doctrine

But however viewed, the doctrine is difficult to understand, very
difficult indeed. The Master K. H., writing to A. P. Sinnett,
said, in the course of a long letter on Buddhism, 'Unless you are
well acquainted with the two tenets Karma and Nirvana—the
double key to the metaphysics of Abhidharma—you will always
find yourself at sea in trying to comprehend the rest . . . Karma
and Nirvana are but two of the seven great MYSTERIES of
Buddhist metaphysics; and but four of the seven are known to the
best Orientalists, and that very imperfectly.'[1] In the Brihad
Upanishad, one of the oldest, Karma is referred to as 'a mighty
secret', and the Buddha himself rebukes Ananda for thinking it
'quite plain of understanding'. 'Say not so, Ananda, say not so.
Deep indeed is this causal law. It is by not understanding, by
not penetrating this doctrine, that this world of men has become
entangled like a ball of twine and unable to pass beyond the
ceaseless round (of rebirth).'[2] If to the greatest mind in history
this doctrine was profound indeed, how shall we, whose eyes
are covered with the dust of ignorance, grasp but the hem of it?
Yet try we must, for it is the Law of laws and governs the whole
universe.

The First Cause is unknowable, for it is beyond the realm of
manifestation and therefore beyond the reach of thought. But
with the appearance of the supreme concept of the One we can
perceive its genesis. When the One becomes two there is
relationship between the two, and in this tension there is action
and reaction. But just as the ABSOLUTE became manifest and
yet remained ABSOLUTE (a dogma which alone makes sense),
so the effect of the FIRST CAUSE is yet unaffected. As Proclus
wrote, 'Everything that is caused both remains in its cause and
proceeds from its cause, and moreover turns back again to its
cause.'[3] But when these causes multiply, and with them their

[1] *The Mahatma Letters to A. P. Sinnett*, p. 110.
[2] Shortened from Woodward: *Some Sayings of the Buddha*, p. 213.
[3] Quoted by Victor Gollancz in *From Darkness to Light*, p. 179.

effects, we have what Sri Krishna Prem calls a vertical polarity,[1] all the effects interrelated as sons of the same father, effects of the same unknowable CAUSE.

What is Karma

We can approach Karma through the law of change. This has no exceptions. *All* is changing, including every single ingredient in the thing we call man, and Karma has been described, I think, by that great writer, Phiroz Mehta, as the mode of change. It therefore applies to all parts of the whole, the One, and preserves the cosmic harmony. What is it? After thirty years' study I accept it as 'The Ultimate Law of the Universe, the source, origin and fount of all other laws which exist throughout Nature. Karma is the unerring law which adjusts effect to cause, on the physical, mental and spiritual planes of being. As no cause remains without its due effect from greatest to least, from a cosmic disturbance down to the movement of your hand, and as like produces like, Karma is that unseen and unknown law which adjusts wisely, intelligently and equitably each effect to its cause, tracing the latter back to its producer. Though itself unknowable, its action is perceivable.'[2]

In my *Zen Buddhism*[3] I have commented on a very early example of what Zen Buddhists call Satori. Two famous Brahmans, contemporaries of the Buddha, sought the essence of his teaching. The summary given by Assaji, a famous disciple of the Buddha, is most illuminating.

'The Buddha hath the cause described
Of all things springing from a cause;
And also how things cease to be—
This is the Great One's Teaching.'

This was enough for the questioner, who then and there attained the 'spotless Dharma-eye' by which to see the essence of things and of that which lies beyond them. 'Coming to be, coming to be; ceasing to be, ceasing to be', so the magic jingle runs, and in it is the whole process of the universe.

[1] *The Yoga of the Kathopanishad*, p. 94.
[2] H. P. Blavatsky: *The Key to Theosophy*, p. 201.
[3] p. 169.

In the moral realm this is the law of retribution—'As ye sow, so shall ye also reap'—yet it is much more than cosmic accountancy. For Karma creates nothing, nor the cause its effect. It is man who creates the causes, and the law adjusts the effects as the restoration of harmony. If the bough of a tree is bent down forcibly, and in springing back should break the arm that held it, shall any complain? There was a painful consequence for a foolish act, no God to punish. We are, or should be, masters of the law, not servants; we are punished by our sins, not for them. The law, then, is the law of harmony in that it operates solely to restore equilibrium when disturbed, and at the expense of the disturber. The effect is the price paid by the causer for the disturbance produced by the cause; it is inherent in the cause and the price admits no argument. Here there is justice and no more. Yet life is One and its parts are inseverable. For the individual to feel with his fellows in their reaping of consequence is compassion, and compassion too is harmony. As I have said elsewhere, 'Only he who sees that law and justice and mercy and love are so many aspects of that Law of harmony will understand that Karma is only a name we give that Law.'[1]

As Cosmic law

If Karma exists it must function on all planes of manifestation, from the cosmic to the growth of a flower. Here we are primarily concerned with the human level, but we cannot consider it alone. For the universe is an inseverable unit, and we cannot consider its parts save as parts of the One of which it is the visible child. It follows that all the universe has moved into causation when I raise my hand, and I affect all living things —and there is nothing dead—when I do it. For 'Buddhism holds that nothing was created singly or individually. All things in the universe—matter and mind—arose simultaneously, all things in it depending on one another, the influence of each mutually permeating and thereby making a universal symphony of harmonious totality. If one item were lacking, the universe would not be complete; without the rest, one item cannot be.'[2]

[1] *Karma and Rebirth*, p. 30.
[2] Takakusu: *The Essentials of Buddhist Philosophy*, p. 40.

The two views of Karma, the individual and the cosmic, are complementary, and are found in the two main Buddhist schools. In the Theravada the emphasis is introvert and individual, although its exponents are hard put at times to maintain an equal emphasis on the individual and on the fact that no such thing exists. In the Mahayana, extension replaces intensity, and Karma becomes the law of cosmic harmony. In the Mahayana, says Dr Suzuki,[1] 'the net of the universe spreads out both in time and space from the centre known as "my self", where it is felt that all the sins of the world are resting on his own shoulders. To atone for them he is determined to subject himself to a system of moral and spiritual training which he considers would cleanse him of all impurities, and by cleansing him cleanse also the whole world of all its demerits.' Indeed this great writer considers that the distinction between the two schools may be summarized under its difference in the treatment of the Karma-conception.

But if all is one, all beings part of it, compassion is a flame that burns in the heart of all aware of it. This inward urge to serve and save is the outer expression of the One in the Many, the recognition in action of the inseverable unity of us all. It works to restore the harmony disturbed by acts which ruffled its repose. It *is* that harmony. Compassion is indeed no attribute, no facet of a complex mind; 'It is the Law of Laws—eternal Harmony; a shoreless universal essence, the light of ever-lasting right and fitness of all things, the law of Love eternal.'[2] As such it is the healing aspect of the karmic law, healing division and the countless wounds of self.

On such a plane of understanding is born the concepts of atonement (at-one-ment) for the acts of the many by the acts of one, and of the deliberate 'turning over' of merit for the benefit of a larger self, or of the Self which is in one sense common to all. Hence, too, the salvation of the part by that 'Other Power' which is the whole, which is the faith of the Pure Land school of Buddhism. Here is a home of that Prajna-consciousness which the Zen devotee is determined to find within; yet within or without, whether Self-or Other-Power, this plane of

[1] *Essays in Zen Buddhism*, Second Series, p. 241.
[2] *The Voice of the Silence*.

pure compassion is a land of No-Karma, for here Karma, caused and suffered by the unit, is digested and subsumed by all. The false antithesis between my karma and yours, between that of the community helped by me or of me as a unit crushed by the follies of the State, is dissolved in the cosmic process of 'coming-to-be' and 'ceasing-to-be', and distinctions between the cause and effect of the parts and the whole are perceived as distinctions born of illusion.

As human law

From such a vision let us return to man and his pain-producing follies. For the unit of right acting is you and me, compact with error, blind with unawareness, and in one sense utterly unreal; yet we are real to this extent, that only by acting rightly shall we ever be cured of our unreality! Let us take heart for we can, to an extent of our own determining, help ourselves and the very universe, or hinder equally. 'No man', wrote H. P. Blavatsky, 'can rise superior to his individual failings without lifting, be it ever so little, the whole body of which he is an integral part. In the same way no one can sin, nor suffer the effects of sin, alone.'[1]

But Karma, though the Law of Laws, is compound in its effects, and may be analysed, at least as to its field of incidence. It includes, from the viewpoint of the human actor, at least five categories. 1. All past actions which have contributed to the present situation. These may be remembered in part, and in part sink into the unconscious, but memory of all is recoverable by the sage. 2. All present actions and reactions arising from past actions. 3. All future actions, which will be caused by present conditions and actions. 4. The mind of the actor as affected by past actions; now by its actions it is causing the acts of a day unborn. 5. The harmony, of the mind and of the All-mind disturbed by this action, and the actor's involvement in its just and delicate restoration.

We are our Karma

From this it is a short step to see how in truth we *are* Karma, our own because it has gathered about the momentary vortex

[1] *The Key to Theosophy*, p. 202.

I   GAUTAMA THE BUDDHA

This Image of the Buddha in meditation came from Buddha Gaya, the site of the Enlightenment. It is of the fourth century A.D. and is now in the National Museum of India.

2. Love in Action. A White Tara, the Goddess of Compassion. Note the extra eyes in the forehead, hands and feet, indicating the all-seeing compassion to help all suffering.

This modern photograph by the Chinese artist, Chang Yin-Chuan, speaks for itself. The Author bought the print at the London Salon of Photography in 1936.

4

ACTION AND REACTION

The Monk, the Gong and the Sound are One. He who disturbs the silence is destroyed in the sound which follows, but is reborn in the ensuing harmony. From a photograph by the Author in Sojiji in Japan in 1946, first reproduced in his *Via Tokyo*

RIGHT ACTION

'Hear no Evil, Speak no Evil, See no Evil'

This is the original carving from which the world-famous phrase originates. It is of the early seventeenth century, and is to be found over the Stables in the compound of the Iyeyasu Shrine at Nikko, Japan.

6   RIGHT IN ACTION

This famous Chinese painting, 'Busy being Idle', is by Mao Ho-Chih of the Sung Dynasty. It calls for no comment save that Right Idleness is an art of which the West has need.

7   DIRECT ACTION

This contribution by Dr D. T. Suzuki to the Author's auto-graph book while in Japan reads, from top to bottom, 'The Power of non-Deception'. Perhaps there is no more to be said.

The photograph is reproduced from the Author's *Zen Buddhism*.

8   NON-ACTION

'Seek in the Impersonal for the Eternal Man'

A Drawing in sepia by Mrs Christmas Humphreys. The design is founded on the twelve Signs of the Zodiac, and with the twelve-petalled Lotus which 'appears' at the centre, might be described as a geometric Mandala. The quotation is from *The Voice of the Silence*, as translated by 'H.P.B.'.

in the river of life called self. 'All that we are', says the *Dham-mapada*, 'is the result of what we have thought. It is founded on our thoughts and made up of our thoughts.' Or in the Sutta Nipata, 'By Karma the world exists, by Karma mankind exists; beings are bound by Karma as the wheels of the rolling cart are held by the linch-pin.' The Buddhist scriptures are full of such quotations, and this truth, profoundly though it may affect all Western thinking, is surely beyond argument. Religious belief or faith, ignoring evidence and reason, may teach otherwise. The wise man sees, with cool appraising eyes, that we are what we have done; we shall be what we do. If so, there is truth in Thackeray's observation: 'Sow a thought, reap an act; sow an act, reap a habit; sow a habit, reap character; sow character and reap destiny.'

Is Karma cause/effect?

So far we have taken Karma as equivalent to cause/effect, on the moral plane of the individual, on the cosmic plane of inter-related consequence too complex for the brain to follow. This may seem sufficient for the day's enquiry into why we are what we are, and what we shall be. But there is an interesting movement in science and in the present world of Theravada Buddhism, of which neither knows of the other, to eschew the concept of causation in favour of some wider relationship. Philosophers speak of many relations which cannot be described as causal, and C. G. Jung has been constrained to invent his theory of 'synchronicity' to explain the sequence of events he cannot accept as caused. At the same time the purist of the southern school of Buddhism, plunging deep into the mine of psychological wisdom known as the Abhidhamma, comes to the same conclusion as the scientist as to the 'discrete flow' of separate thoughts or events or moments of consciousness. 'This being so, that becomes; this ceasing, that ceases.' Each this and that is a separate entity for a moment of time, and by its nature gives in dying birth to another. Analogies are used, the impulse of the sea which presses water in one place to rise into a wave, from which arises another wave, and another; the light of a candle used to light a sequence of others—is each light 'caused' by the last? But why not call this cause and effect if the effect would not be so without the cause? Because, it is argued, if cause and effect are equal and opposite, as science used to say, then the whole event is consumed when the effect follows the cause, and there is no running on. Why not? Of course the effect is consumed in its cause, and the cause in its effect. The cause and effect are one thing viewed differently. But no one cause is single, being the combination of a thousand 'conditions' or causes; and each effect is in turn the father of a thousand more. Who can single out one wave in the sea, or speak of a portion of the wind that blows one leaf about the garden? Buddhist philosophers speak of the four views on cause/effect which alone are possible, that they are identical, different, identical and different, neither identical nor different, but what bearing has this on the Law and its visible operation? We are here concerned, let it be said again, with right acting, and not with doctrine save as it helps to that end. Does it help to expand the tremendous saying quoted by Assaji into the famous twelve Nidanas? That all things spring from a cause, and with the dying of the cause the effects die too—is this not enough? For those in need of them, the spokes of this Wheel of Becoming, the cycle of Dependent Origination, the progress of this Causal Sequence (as Professor Takakusu was content to call it)[1] are available for study and meditation, but for working purposes is Marcus Aurelius not sufficient? 'Subsequents follow antecedents by bond of inner consequence. And just as things existent exhibit harmonious co-ordination, so things coming into being display not bare succession but a marvellous internal relationship.' This relationship is no less than oneness, as one would expect of the Law of laws. As Alan Watts points out, 'We do not sweat because it is hot; the sweating is the heat.' Cause and effect are one; by reason of our infirmities of spiritual sight we see them separately. Yet of the two, the cause is paramount, for it is this aspect of the act that is under our immediate control. It is therefore better to concentrate on causes, for when the causing is right the right effect must follow. This causation is in the mind, and the motive is of vast importance. Better it is to act with the right intention and to suffer the consequence of error than to act for evil though the event should turn out well. For

[1] *The Essentials of Buddhist Philosophy*, p. 30.

the intent is itself an act in the mind, and on a plane where consequence is swifter, stronger and wider-reaching than action in the heavier substance of our clay.

We are not the puppets of our past behaviour. Karma is not destiny. The opposition of freedom to law is a false antithesis, for though the present is determined by the past the future is always free. But the past is heavy with our foolish causes, and in the present we must receive the effects. Yet now we are different from the man that sowed the seed; so is our circumstance made different from our recent causing. Now we may act as we please in our reaction, and create anew, save this, that sometimes the volume and momentum of our past causation is too heavy and too instant to be neutralized. There are times when there is nothing wiser to be done than to take it, and absorb it, and be free.

Equating cause and effect

The complications of the law are infinite, but, like so much of Eastern teaching, easier to understand in the act of experience. If all that we do is a cause which bears an effect, and this applies to each Karma-producing unit on the globe, what then of chance, or luck or coincidence? When I take an unusual street to the station, and in it meet some friend I had not met for twenty years who 'happened' to pass that way for the first time in his life, and we meet and part, was the meeting coincidence, just chance? Or was it the net resultant of a million causes in our several lives which brought us two together? And is all suffering earned and merited? When ten are hurt in a train crash and I am one of them, was there cause in my past action for my being hurt? Or did I but bear my part in the general injury from a general and other cause? And if but part of my woe and happiness is self-produced, and part of it but the effect of causing by a larger unit, as a shipwreck or in war, where do I draw the line? I do not know, and opinions, for what they are worth, must widely differ.

The truth is that it is quite impossible to equate any cause/effect beyond trivialities. If I lose my temper and cause an injury I soon perceive the consequence of the act, and as a magistrate I sometimes point out to a prisoner that it is he that sends himself to prison and not I; but this is a low view of a cosmic principle. When all is One in essence our intercausation must be infinite in subtely, and even the labels we attach to Karma are our own. 'There is nothing either good or bad but thinking makes it so', and there is no such thing as bad Karma or good. Nor can we interfere with another's Karma, as so many new to the doctrine falsely believe. If it is right to help one's neighbour in some way, it is right, and it is part of his Karma that he is so helped. The good Samaritan has come down through history as the pattern of right action. Would he have done so had he argued, 'It was the consequence of this man's error that he should be robbed and left to die; it is no concern of mine'? As already quoted from *The Voice of the Silence*, 'Inaction in a deed of mercy is action in a deadly sin', and when compassion calls for action it is never wise to refuse.

How, then, does Karma act on the individual in its adjustment for past deeds? Surely the main effect is on mind and character. It may be true that 'He that draws the sword shall perish by the sword', but the result of evil action goes deeper than injury to the same effect. Each second of time we are acting in thought, in the sense of habitual thought and feeling and consequent course of action. Evil coarsens the mind and the quality of thinking, and evil thoughts breed evil deeds. So the downward course is a spiral, as it might be upward with well-chosen thoughts and deeds, and all the world suffers or is lifted in the Law's adjusted consequence.

Do we learn by suffering? We do, but slowly. Yet suffering does not wipe out the Karma that caused it, it does but tell us that the cause was bad. The pain draws attention to error. We seek for the cause and if we are wise remove it. For this is the light and hope of the Law in action, that we may use it as we will. Though a man is the product of his causing, Karma, says a Buddhist scripture, 'is his means of going beyond'. By the deliberate change of thought-habit, character may be changed for the better in remarkably short time. By change of thought comes change of reaction to events and circumstance. By such a change the man digests his own past karma at whatever cost of suffering, and is then free to affect his future and to remould this 'sorry scheme of things' just so much nearer to his heart's desire.

Man has the privilege, says Dr Suzuki[1] of being aware of his Karma-bondage, and this privilege, implying freedom, gives him the power to transcend his bonds. By accepting our Karma, and the suffering that such bravery involves, we prepare ourselves for the sacrifice of self. But even Self, in the sense used in this study, is bound in Karma, and this too must go before we can be free. What is the answer to this problem? It lies, says Dr Suzuki in the realm of no-Karma, and this can be reached by the utter acceptance of things as they are. Only so can we contact that element of the Unthinkable which lies beyond thought, as the intuition arises when reason is known to have failed. Only by the birth of an awareness beyond cause/effect may both be transcended, when, bound in effects felt alien to our selves, we feel for and become the Law. Then only, at the 'still centre of the turning world', we shall be free of the Law while moving with it happily. He who is love need use no loving; he that is Law is in all things cause/effect and free.

---

[1] *The Essence of Buddhism*, pp. 26-9.

Chapter 9

Action and Interaction

Ultimately, nothing is irrelevant to anything else. There is a togetherness of all things in an endless hierarchy of living and interacting patterns.

ALDOUS HUXLEY, Adonis and the Alphabet[1]

IN the 'Actor and his Circumstance' we saw the unceasing interaction between these two ever-changing knots in the flow of life. In 'Action and Reaction' we saw this nexus as, generally speaking, causal, with its ambit the entire universe. Let us now consider the actor in his relation to his fellow actors individually, and to humanity in the mass. As Karma is the law of adjustment of the reaction to each actor of his act, so each human must adjust himself to each other human whom he affects and who affects him. This adjustment should in the ideal be precise and perfect. It is seldom so, and when the maladjustment is severe a crisis develops, first in the mind and then in action, leading often to violence and crime. So important is this adjustment that psychiatrists who seek to heal the lack of it, submit themselves in the course of their training to mental analysis by an older expert in order that no such tensions shall remain in a mind that, to be useful, must be poised, serene, unshakeable.

First we must face this larger field of circumstance. Just as we take our karma as it comes, so we must accept our family, colleagues, friends and enemies, and adjust ourselves to each new contact. Only a constant self-adjustment will produce that mastery of Karma which alone will end it as a barrier on the way. 'I follow my karma as it moves, with perfect contentment', said the Master Ryokwan, which is an ideal accom-

[1] Op. cit., pp. 193–4.

plishment. In striving to do so we shall either stress relations with individuals or with the larger unit of class or group or the vague unhappy unit that we call mankind. The choice will depend on our mental make-up, but as the mass is the individual writ largely it has no ultimate importance. To each and to all we have our duty; to all alike we should give, of help of all kinds, of truth at the highest we can reach, and the supreme gift of understanding. The basis of this duty is the fact, no sentimental vision but a fact in nature, of brotherhood.

Brotherhood

The 'Father' of our brotherhood is of course the Absolute, as all that we may know of it, the One. From 'the Unborn, the Incomposite, the Unmade' come all of us, and all things born. It follows that the higher we move in consciousness, the nearer to the source of that ceaseless motion we call matter, the closer we are to that Mind of which all minds are part, and hence the closer to each other. It is by reason of our oneness with the source that we are one with each other, and all mystical awareness of such oneness has a rational and metaphysical basis. As R. H. Blyth puts it, 'The closer we are to the Mind the closer we are to persons', and much follows, for as we appreciate the One in all things we more and more appreciate each other. For the first time, perhaps, we see our fellow men as other versions of ourselves, and we look at them. Without prejudice, without uncalled-for love or hate, we look at them and find them interesting, as worth at least attention and respect. We feel with them, rejoice in their joy, and suffer with them in the true meaning of compassion, 'And in my brother's face I see my own unanswered agony.'

But this is an ideal view. For a while we fight with them, and all of them, and will do so for so long as there is not room for their desires and our desires to be equally fulfilled at once. When a million minds are moving on the same plane in a million separate directions, some will get where they want and what they want, and others will not, and complain. But if we are willing to be pushed around, claim nothing, are content to be ordinary and no one in particular, we shall soon be past hurting. Indeed, as self ebbs out the Void pours in, and the

107

Void being nothing is also everything. 'Foregoing self, the Universe grows I.' But this self-control, most puzzling to our friends, must be of the mind as well. For we people the world about us with our thoughts and desires, our fancies, complaints and resentment. We shall not come to terms with the entities about us if many of them are the waste products of our own unguarded minds projected onto the personalities of our unwitting neighbours.

But as we let go of self we shall lose the chains of our self-wrought karma. The good we do, not done for self, will flow into the wide impersonal stream of cosmic purpose, and will not need us to receive the consequences. And hating no man we shall earn no hate, but make every man our teacher. 'Enter into every man's inner Self; and let every man enter into thine', said the Emperor Marcus Aurelius, but the Greek slave Epictetus was the more practical. 'Learn my mind—show me yours; then go and say that you met me. Let us try each other; if I have a wrong principle, rid me of it; if you have, out with it. That is what meeting a philosopher means.' Are all the Stoics dead today?

Love, friendship and compassion

From brotherhood is born love, friendship and compassion, here taken as different from each other as the body, soul and spirit of St Paul. For love is but the reverse of hate, an attraction that may have been and may become a repulsion equally strong. It is of the earth earthy and has no lasting quality. It is excellent material for poetry, films and the perpetuation of the species, but it binds in all its actions, and the binding factor is the self. How much nobler is friendship, that wants nothing and gives all, that puts the other's self before its own, that is beyond the domination of sex, or age or rivalry. Here the bridge between the two is at the level of equality as fellow humans, as facets of one Mind. Here Self is unaffected by the foolish deeds of self, and when these are communicated, on the evil wings of gossip, the friend may regret, if he stoops to believe them, yet the friendship remains unchanged. Friendship worthy of the name is recognition, from previous lives if the Buddhist doctrine be accepted—certainly from recognition of the spiritual factor common to all which is seen in action in the movements of one's friend. But its real value is in the lowering of battlements. Only friends can afford to remove the mask, the 'persona' or personality through which we view and are viewed by the world. Only with friends can one afford to be old and tired and selfish; or despondent or ashamed. But if two can meet together, each with his dull impediments, admitting the unregenerate factors of the self as such, how much can they help one another in the common task of dropping self, becoming Self, and aiming even to drop that too, at the level of Prajna-vision, in primordial Oneness?

Yet higher than this is compassion, which flows from enlightenment and is inseparable from it. The Buddha's teaching is based on the twin pillars of Prajna, wisdom and Karuna, compassion, and the two are one. One cannot acquire wisdom and then cultivate compassion; one cannot by the exercise of compassion develop its counterpart. The wise man loves his fellow men and works for their release from ignorance; the man of heart is wise in his compassion.

There is no source for such compassion. It is not the divine pity of any God. 'It is not', as Dr Suzuki says, 'a solid body from which love emanates or issues towards objects, but it is the feeling of self-identity flowing through an eternal process of becoming.'[1] This feeling of self-identity is both rational and mystical. The mind says it must be so; the heart says it is, and in this synthesis is the higher third of the intuition which, acting beyond distinctions, sees the Self as one in many and acts accordingly.

But the word compassion, or its Greek equivalent, sympathy, means to feel with, and this implies a feeling with and a suffering of another's sorrow. For in 'that mighty sea of sorrow formed of the tears of men' all humans are submerged, and he who keeps his garments dry of it ignores his own mind in his ignorance of his neighbours'. Buddhism is not a 'cold' religion because it is not founded on emotion. Nor is the surgeon 'cold' who with a mind cleansed of emotion acts from the level of cool awareness and appraisal. So does the Buddhist, self-trained to perceive the One in the many, and the follies of the many and of each of

[1] *The Essence of Buddhism*, Second edition, p. 47.

them born of the same ignorance. Compassion is beyond emotion, and the attraction/repulsion with which all emotion disturbs the mind. Yet it is not impersonal, as science is impersonal, for the Buddhist is one who moves to the Goal achieved by an earlier man in history, Gautama the Buddha, a goal to be achieved at the end of time by all. Each fellow human is therefore a friend, known as such or as yet unknown, whose eyes are windows of the same Enlightenment, whose feet are treading the same Path to the Goal. There are paradoxes in all compassionate action. The Self helps brother Self to destroy all sense of separateness, to make real the knowledge that even Self is unreal, being but a bundle of changing attributes and qualities that in the end will cease to be this or that or anything at all. But at present my Self is trying to purge itself of the undesirable, because Light-obscuring factors in the total man that is labelled with my name. Your Self is doing the same. 'Work out your own salvation, with diligence', said the Buddha. In trying to do so it is my privilege, and duty, to help you to work out yours. My duty, because compassion, as Wisdom applied, must act and act unceasingly, whether as visible help or as mental healing, or at least as the spiritual force exerted on all that lives by a man who lives his own life wholly, naturally, contented with things as they are because he made them so, and as they will be until he succeeds in making them better.

Yet we cannot wait for compassion to be born with the coming of Prajna, Wisdom. We must use the strongest force we possess, desire, to bring it to birth. In a powerful passage in his latest work, Dr Suzuki says,[1] 'The Buddhist training consists in transforming Trishna (desire) into Karuna, ego-centred love into something universal, eros into agape.' He goes on to quote from the Master Joshu, who was asked, 'Could Buddha cherish desires (Klesa)?' He answered, 'Yes, he decidedly has them.' Asked, 'How could that be?' the Master replied, 'His desire is to save the whole universe.' I once wrote somewhere, 'We all serve self, but our place in evolution may be measured by the size of the self we serve.' It may be expanded from me to my family, my nation and to all mankind; or it may remain at me.

[1] *Mysticism, Christian and Buddhist*, p. 73.

The key to compassion in action is surely this, to concern ourselves with the Self in others, and to ignore their self. We all have mental clothes and habits and possessions of which we are ashamed; we are in process of shedding them. If we see but the best in others they may come to overlook our worst. Hence the evil of gossip which is solely concerned with the worst in all of us. Why do we take such pleasure in stabbing at the faults in others, thereby making them more sore? Why, when we wish to be better, do we maliciously hinder the total progress of us all? I know not, but we do.

Compassion sacrifices self to Self and strives to lay Self on the altar of SELF. But surely, we talk much nonsense about sacrifice. The thing we sacrifice is self, and its needs and petty desires. But how clever of us! Why lament the loss? For what suffers in the act is self, the ingredients of us that we long to destroy. Do we moan when we part with rubbish, lament or boast when we throw away the no-longer-loved accumulation of the years? Surely when the heart of compassion is wakened, because wisdom begins to illumine the mind, we shall agree with the Lama in Talbot Mundy's *Om*, 'There is no such thing as sacrifice—there is only opportunity to serve.' We may even agree with *The Voice of the Silence*, 'To live to benefit mankind is the first step. To practise the six glorious virtues is (but) the second.' If we ask why, we are answered. If all is One, compassion is indeed a law whose essence is harmony, and when that harmony is confused, it is Karma that adjusts the effects to causes, but compassion that heals the heart that caused the confusion. What, then, is the answer when Karuna whispers in the would-be Bodhisattva's ear? Compassion speaks and saith: 'Can there be bliss when all that lives must suffer? Shalt thou be saved and hear the whole world cry?'

The unit of Karma is not confined to the individual. There is family, tribal, national Karma, that of the 'whites' against the Red Indians, or of the French and English for the wars they fought in centuries gone by. In the same way a club or society has its Karma, and the 'goodwill' of a business has monetary value. Schools move up and down in reputation; religions must suffer from their past misdeeds; the new management of anything takes over the Karma of the old. It is never quite possible to begin any venture afresh, for the hand of past causes is heavy upon it. The same applies to class and class, and the history of this foolish struggle is a study in the karmic law.

The individual and the mass

But the man is at all times a unit in himself, and he is serving no one when he surrenders his integrity. His relation to the larger self is important, for on this polarity, man and the herd, the individual and the mass, the citizen and the State, is based all civilization. Yet the dominant factor in this bi-polar field is the man. The larger unit of committee, council, parliament exists to serve its members in their several needs, and not otherwise. Man is the universe in miniature; he needs no collectivity in which to express the unlimited wisdom and compassion which dwell in each mind that is part of All-Mind. Thus groups are good as they serve individuals; evil as they steal a false life of their own. All large concerns are potentially evil, for they loose and express the worst aspects of the unconscious, and men in the service of such will do cold-hearted evil that they would not do under torture in their individual lives. As Emerson wrote, 'To educate the wise man the State exists; and with the appearance of the wise man the State expires.' No man was ever saved by the State or any other corporate body. As Kenneth Walker wrote in a memorable passage, 'The hope of mankind does not lie in the action of any corporate body, be it ever so powerful, but in the influence of individual men and women who for the sake of a greater have sacrificed a lesser aim.'[1] It is the business of the State or larger unit to provide the conditions conducive to the proper development of the individual member. Amiel puts it well. 'All that can be expected from the most perfect institutions is that they should make it possible for individual excellence to develop itself, not that they should produce the excellent individual.' Laws can improve conditions; never men. National strife will not cease by the proclamations of nations. Progress is personal, and only the accumulation of personal improvement will improve the state.

The individual must therefore wean himself from reliance on any Other Power, for we have seen and see today the effect

[1] Quoted in Gollancz: *From Darkness to Light*, p. 573.

of the contrary belief in action. He must learn to separate from the tribe in his decisions, though they may and probably will accord with those of the tribe. He will surrender nothing save his right to dominate, to command another to his will. He will co-operate as a free unit, for though his ambition be to be free of self it is he alone who can 'drop it'; none shall take it from him—else he will not be free.

If this applies to all men everywhere, it applies particularly to the Western world today. Dissatisfied with the material claims of science the man of the West is turning within. Yet here again is a false dichotomy. 'Mastery of the inner world', wrote Caryl Baynes,[1] 'with a relative contempt for the outer, must inevitably lead to great catastrophes. Master of the outer world, to the exclusion of the inner, delivers us over to the daemonic forces of the latter and keeps us barbaric despite all outward forms of culture. The solution cannot be found either in deriding Eastern spirituality as impotent, or by mistrusting science as a destroyer of humanity. We have to see that the spirit must lean on science as its guide in the world of reality, and that science must turn to the spirit for the meaning of life.'

Learning and teaching

From all our fellows in all circumstances we learn, or we are fools indeed. And as we learn we teach. 'Point out the Way—however dimly and lost among the host—as does the evening star to those who tread their path in darkness. Give light and comfort to the toiling pilgrim, and seek out him who knows still less than thou.' Thus *The Voice of the Silence*, and the Buddha was an example of the law. Though severely tempted to accept the fruits of a thousand lives of lone endeavour, to enter Parinirvana and to pass from the eyes of men, he went forth into the world and taught, seeking for some at least 'whose eyes would be covered with little dust'. And he taught the Bhikkhus likewise. 'Go ye forth, O Bhikkhus, on your journey, for the profit of the many, for the bliss of the many, out of compassion for the world. Proclaim, O Bhikkhus, the Dhamma, goodly in its beginning, goodly in its middle, goodly in its ending. . . . There will be some who will understand.' It is

---

[1] *The Secret of the Golden Flower*, p. viii.

never difficult to find someone with even less knowledge than oneself, and one who needs the knowledge that one can give. As the blood in the body must flow, as the breath taken in must be given out again, so wisdom gained must be wisdom given— so far as any man may teach another more than to point a way. And of all that we give another the truth is best. Yet 'You yourself must make the effort. (Even) Buddhas do but point the Way.' Truth can be offered, but the other man must be left his freedom to refuse. Truth can be degraded if forced on unwilling minds, and we can certainly cast pearls before swine. This is the Buddhist tolerance, to offer but no more. To offer is our duty; to refuse, his right.

We can teach by example, as the Buddha, as Jesus the Christ, showing forth the Truth by what we are. By this may a teacher be tested, and thus the Ven Sangharakshita proposes a test for Buddhism. 'The sole test of the genuineness of any school of Buddhism is its capacity to produce enlightened beings.'[1] If not for this purpose why does the school exist? But even example can rightly use devices. 'Those who intend to be the teachers of others', said Hui-neng, 'should themselves be skilled in the various expedients which lead others to enlightenment.' But the plane must be that of the intuition. As Jung greatly said, 'a concept is not a carrier of life. The sole and natural carrier of life is the individual, and this holds true throughout nature.' And he quotes from Pestalozzi's work *Ideen* who says that 'None of the institutions or means of education established for the masses and the needs of men in the aggregate serve to advance human culture. Our race develops its human qualities in essence only from face to face, from heart to heart.'[2] Thoughts may be used, and must be used, but only as means of communication of personal experience, and when no better means can be found. Said the Master Huang Po, 'A single thought and you separate yourself from reality. All (empirical) thought is vain, for you cannot use the mind to seek something from mind, nor the Dharma to seek something from the Dharma. There is a tacit understanding and nothing more, for any ordinary mental process leads to error. This understanding is transmitted from mind to mind.'

[1] *A Survey of Buddhism*, p. 212.   [2] *Essays on Contemporary Events*, p. 31.

These truths are the platitudes of Eastern wisdom which from the dawn of history has taught what may be taught of Reality from heart to heart. The teacher or Guru makes no claim. 'The man who claims that he knows, knows nothing; but he who claims nothing, knows.' Offering all that he is and has to those who prove worthy to be taught he exhibits 'that generosity in self-expenditure which is the hall-mark of spiritual leadership'.

He teaches from his own experience, but the pupil takes no more than a working hypothesis, to be tested or rejected by his own experience. The teacher provides the seed; the pupil provides the soil and works at the cultivation. All dogma is an insult to whom it is given, for it robs the receiver of his right to reject, of his right to learn from the consequence of error. But the pupil has his special needs at any stage of the journey, and the teacher should give what is needed and no more. Hence the danger of all general teaching save of general principles. In the East it is personal, the teacher giving to the pupil only what he is satisfied the latter can assimilate and apply. Modern Western history shows the wisdom of this course. The man who knows how to split the atom (and the wise men of the East have secrets quite as powerful), should preserve that knowledge and grant it to none that cannot be trusted to use it solely for beneficent ends. But what a gale of laughter would greet this obvious wisdom in a Western science laboratory! The difference lies between the national will to destroy all rivals, and the personal will to help other persons to En-lightenment.

The wise man learns, then, from another mind, face to face if possible; if not, then from his books. And he should teach the same. Heart to heart is the Self's communion with Self, each as a known expression of the One. If the doctor, the psychiatrist, the priest act singly in their healing, shall the purveyor of the Wisdom, and there is but one, act otherwise? This, then, is the true relation of man to man, as teacher/pupil and tested friend. What stands in the way of it? The self, in each and all. Let us see how in action, by right acting our right action, this self may be destroyed. But first there is a bridge to be surmounted, and a high one.

Chapter 10

Building the Bridge

The end of man is an action and not a thought,
though it were the noblest.   CARLYLE

I HAVE long been fascinated by the gap, sometimes an insurmountable chasm, which exists between theory and practice, resolution and performance, the will and the deed. The annual failure to implement for more than a day or two one's New Year's resolutions is a popular joke, but these vows of reform are usually but lightly made. More serious and more puzzling is such a case as the following. A lecture audience or class of educated, serious-minded persons listen to a talk on some aspect of the inner life. They are collectively and individually interested. They understand the reasons for the desirability of change, in habit or outlook. They desire to make such a change, or to begin to make it. They form an internal resolve to carry out some clearly defined purpose, and they leave the room with every intention of doing it. They do nothing of the kind, and many of them within twenty four hours have forgotten the very resolve.

This failure is more important and more puzzling than mere forgetfulness, or failure to do something which, though vaguely agreed, was never in the forefront of consciousness as something to be done. Nor is it a modern phenomenon. St Paul bewailed the habit; 'For the good that I would I do not, but the evil which I would not, that I do.' It may be that the problem is greater for the West than for the East. 'The difference', says Dr Conze, 'between the Buddhist and the European and American philosophers lies in what they do with a philosophical proposition once they have arrived at it. In Europe we have become accustomed to an almost complete gap between the theory of philosophers and their practice, between their views on the nature of the universe and their mode of life.'[1] Even Buddhist scholars in the West suffer from this sad dichotomy. A famous Pali scholar broke in when I mentioned something about the application of Buddhism. 'How do you mean, "Buddhism applied"? How can you *apply* Buddhism?' If there are those, therefore, who fail to see the gap, how much more difficult is it for those who observe its presence and width to cross it?

A genuine bridge

The crossing must not be complete, in the sense that relationship ceases between either bank of the river. Always we must tread the Middle Way, between spirit and matter, thought and action, direct 'experience' and its manifold forms of expression. We are and must remain what Aldous Huxley calls amphibians, 'living simultaneously in the world of experience and the world of notions, in the world of direct apprehension of Nature, God and ourselves, and the world of abstract verbalized knowledge about these primary facts. Our business as human beings is to make the best of both these worlds.'[2]

But the gap exists, even though it is illusion. 'So far as Buddha-nature is concerned', said the Patriarch Hui-neng, 'there is no difference between an enlightened man and an ignorant one. What makes the difference is that one realizes it while the other does not.' But it is a large difference. 'Look within; thou art Buddha', says *The Voice of the Silence*, but the stream of Samsara, worldly existence, flows wide and deep between our knowledge about that fact and our experience of it.

Such is the gap and we must cross it. Nature does not stand still, nor anything in the whole field of creation. Having reached the bank we must enter the stream or go backwards; there is no remaining still. 'I am the Way, the Truth, the Life', said the voice of the Christ or Buddhic principle within. All true religion is, and living philosophy should be, a way, a way to be trodden, from here and now to whatever the end, if any, may prove to be. 'In Buddhism', said the late Professor Takakusu most pithily, 'religion is understood as the practical

[1] *Buddhism*, p. 20.   [2] *Adonis and the Alphabet*, p. 15.

application of the philosophic doctrine.' 'By their fruits ye shall know them', indeed, or, in the poetic diction of the *Dhamma-pada*, 'Like a beautiful flower, full of colour but without scent, are the fine and fruitless words of one who does not act accordingly.' 'Beliefs are rules for action', said William James in his *Varieties of Religious Experience*, or as Mr Kenneth Walker puts it, 'To know more a man must become more'.

The Buddhist position is dogmatic if in this alone, that Buddhism is the Way by which the individual achieves the Enlightenment which made one man, Gautama Siddhartha, the Buddha, the Awakened One. 'All Buddhist teachings', says Dr Suzuki, 'are the outcome of a warm heart cherished for all sentient beings, and not of a cold intellect which tries to unveil the secrets of existence by logic. That is to say, Buddhism is personal experience and not impersonal philosophy.'[1] In brief, 'As he speaks so he does; as he does so he speaks. Therefore is he called Tathagata.'[2] The necessity to bridge the gap is therefore apparent. The difficulty of doing so is equally apparent to most of us, and one story of this difficulty will suffice. In the T'ang Dynasty of China the governor of a Province, himself a well-known poet, called on a Zen Master living in his province and asked him, 'What is the teaching of Buddhism?' The Master replied with the famous Buddhist quatrain:

> 'Cease to do evil,
> Learn to do good.
> Cleanse your own heart—
> This is the teaching of the Buddhas.'

The Governor protested, 'Any child of three knows that.' 'Any child of three may know it' replied the Master, 'but even an old man of eighty finds it difficult to practise.'[3]

It is hardly surprising, therefore, that the number who practise what they preach, or even what they believe is comparatively few. Hence the famous outcry of the Stoic Greek slave, Epictetus. 'What, then, is a Stoic, in the sense that we call that a statue of Phidias which is modelled after that master's

---

[1] *Essays in Zen Buddhism*, Third Series, p. 178.
[2] '*He who travels in the footsteps of his predecessors*', see *Digha Nikaya*, III, 135.
[3] Suzuki: *Essays in Zen Buddhism*, Third Series, p. 376.

art? Show me a man in this sense modelled after the doctrines ever on his lips. Show me a man that is sick, and happy; in danger, and happy; on his death-bed, and happy; in evil report, and happy! Show me him, I ask again. So help me, Heaven, I long to see one Stoic!'

As applied to the West the problem, then, is to fuse the divided types of follower and scholar into a third type, that I have called elsewhere a 'schollower'. The one knows, but his knowledge is sterile; the other, knowing but little, strives to apply and teach what he knows. The ideal man is both, but he is rare indeed.

The cause of the gap

If it is true, then, that 'no truth is understood until applied', why does such a gap exist; what is the cause of it? Wiser minds than mine have given the subject thought, and in the long history of man's development have no doubt offered many an answer. For myself I know but three. The first is the quality of inertia, to be found in all forms of matter, from a stationary motor car to a habit of mind. Whether the force is needed to change a direction of thought, or to move the car from rest, it is the same inertia, the dead weight of resistance to change, which impedes and may neutralize the force applied. If the strength of will is increased to a point when it is greater than the power of inertia, there will be movement, and one of the ingredients in bridging the gap is therefore a stronger will than that which has failed to bridge it. Of the technique of 'raising the head of steam' as a friend describes his exercises before attempting to solve a koan, more will be said later.

Secondly, there may be dissipation of the energy in hand. If a man has a hundred units of energy, for example, and spends ten on each of ten activities he will not leap some difficult gap which needs, say, ninety units, whereas a man who has concentrated the whole of his hundred on that single task will succeed.

We in the West habitually fritter away a large percentage of our energy in useless physical movements, in emotional reactions of annoyance, impatience and fear, and in a perpetual 'chatter' of fruitless thinking. When we need all our units for a single act we complain of 'nervous exhaustion', for where body and emotions and mind are alike in unending though useless activity, what 'head of steam' is left for the activity we really want to perform?

More serious still, and perhaps including the other two, is the evil of divided motive. We think that we want to do this thing 'with the whole soul's will', but the mind is divided against itself. Consciously, we genuinely want to do it; unconsciously we don't. How, then, when the horse-power of the car is harnessed to two sets of transmission at the same time, will the car move strongly and well in either direction? Consider the word, alignment. Engineers are concerned to apply to movement the maximum of the power available. They strive to eliminate all wasted effort and friction, and to transmit from the source of power to the purpose of the machine the maximum force, by way of the most perfect alignment. In a car, from explosion of gas to movement of cylinder, and so through divers crank shafts and the like to the axle and the movement of the wheels on the road; or in the Self, from unconscious to conscious desire, through will, thought, motive, emotion, via divers 'devices' or means to the physical and visible end, the ideal process is as swift and wasteless as the flash of lightning. In the human process a large percentage of the effort available is usually wasted, and often converted into heat (of temper) and the wear and tear of the whole machinery. But if this applies to any one act, how much more when the man is attempting several wasteful actions at the same time?

If this be right, then the way to bridge the gap is to develop more will-power, to overcome thereby the quality of laziness or inertia, to conserve and concentrate the energy thus produced and to align the whole machinery of our being so that every effort produces the maximum of the desired result. But is this right; would this be sufficient, even if we knew how to do it all? It would not, and we secretly know it. The strength which will bridge the gap will not come out of will-power or any of the faculties in the individual man. We must, in Trine's immortal phrase, attach our belts to the power-house of the Universe, so that the alignment of force is not from my will, but from Will, not from my mind but from Mind, or whatever capital letters we like to use for the force of the Whole of which we are each an infinitesimally small but entirely necessary part. In Buddhist terms we must acquire the faculty of Prajna, supreme Wisdom, the awareness of that Non-duality which lies behind the Many and the One, which, being Uncreate, is above or behind or at the heart of all aspects of creation. We must acknowledge and surmount the empire of the opposites, raise consciousness above the limitations of thought and all its concept-minions, drop the barrier of wrong belief and above all of 'self' and then, waiting in humbleness of heart quite suddenly see—that the Seeker and the Sought are one, that action is but the form of being, and that all that is done is utterly and absolutely right. But *how*?

In a way there is no how, for we cannot command this ultimate and sole worthwhile experience. In a way the harder we seek it the less we shall find; we cannot understand the Truth. We can but train ourselves, clean ourselves and prepare ourselves that our minds may be in readiness to 'see'. Truly, 'the readiness is all', and the experience will come to those who are watchful in the night. Its power will be proportionate to the lack of obstacles which stand between.

But how to prepare, to empty ourselves of self? Not by scriptures, ritual or textbook courses, nor by religion in the sense of that shield against feared experience which Jung so fiercely attacks;[1] nor yet by the invocation of some Other Power to which we plead to save us from our sins. Rather we shall find it by getting out of the way. To that end we can study the self which stands in the way and choose our means to be rid of it. This path we shall tread for seven days a week. If we drop purpose from our mind's curriculum, and treat it for itself alone, we shall the more rapidly remove the treader of the path. Soon, there will only be a walking on, but the experience will grow of a joy untellable, of a mind that, alighting nowhere is unmovable, and of a compassion infinite for the littlest living thing. The following are but notes for that achievement.

[1] *Psychology and Religion*, pp. 52-3.

PART II

Into Action

Chapter 11

The Ways to the One

*Buddha's teaching is adjusted to the need of the
taught as the medicine of the skilled physician
is to the malady of the patient.... The indeter-
minacy of the Absolute allows freedom of
approach; numberless are the ways by which it
could be reached. The sole condition is that the
method chosen should suit the disciple's disposi-
tion; this is the doctrine of Upaya-Kausalya
(excellence in the choice of means), and it applies
to every doctrine.*

T. R. V. MURTI

*The Path is one for all; the means to reach the
Goal must vary with the Pilgrims.*

THE VOICE OF THE SILENCE

THE end is One, but in the words of a Buddhist proverb,
'The ways to the One are as many as the lives of men.' A way
must be chosen, and trodden firmly to its end. It may be that
where I am and where I would be are both illusion, as all
distinction between them, but, to quote again the Patriarch
Hui-neng, 'So far as Buddha-nature is concerned there is no
difference between an enlightened man and an ignorant one.
What makes the difference is that one realizes it while the other
does not.'[1] This 'realization' is a matter of direct experience,
and the experience comes to a mind made ready for it. The
preparation of the mind is a process of training, and the process
is itself the way. That it must be trodden and not merely discussed is by now, it is hoped, an axiom in the reader's mind.
Yet too many would-be arrivers at the Goal are adept in the
discussion of means of attaining it and, like a man in an arm-chair
at a cross-roads whence five roads diverge, they speak with
skill on the merits of all, but rise to begin the journey upon

[1] *The Sutra of Wei Lang*, p. 27.

125

none of them. True, if a method or way is found to be incorrect for that person at that time, let a change be made, but not for the sake of change. One does not change from a careful choice of dwelling, or method of learning golf, or even the reading of a book, without giving it a fair trial. The problem is often to know what is wanted, and the same applies to choosing a Way. There are thousands of thinking minds adrift in the West today that wander unhappily from meeting to meeting and book to book, looking for what they know not, but too often for a method of reaching the goal without effort or payment or exchange of any kind.

The choice of way

The chosen way must be that which is right for you now. It may not be right for you later, or for others now. In his commentary on the Secret of the Golden Flower, Richard Wilhelm quotes the Book of the Elixir as saying, 'When the right man makes use of wrong means, the wrong means work in the right way. But if the wrong man uses the right means, the right means work in the wrong way.' This refers to the conservation of the seed (of sex), but in his own Commentary on the text Dr C. G. Jung says of the latter part of the saying, 'This Chinese saying stands in sharp contrast to our belief in the "right" method irrespective of the man who applies it. In reality when it comes to things like these, everything depends on the man and little or nothing on the method. The latter is only the way and direction laid down by a man in order that his action may be the true expression of his nature.'[1] The need and purpose of tolerance is therefore obvious. We seldom have the means of knowing what is best for our nearest and dearest; more rarely still what is right for those we scarcely know. And in any event what time have we to spare from our own path to advise, unsolicited, the right way for others?

In the ideal not only the Goal should be visible but all the steps on the ladder in between. This is seldom achieved, and most climbers belong to one or other of the types which have been described as the mystic or the occultist. The former, in this distinction, has seen a glimpse of the distant Goal, and its

[1] *The Secret of the Golden Flower*, pp. 69-70 and 79.

light still burns, however dimly, in his eyes. The occultist is the scientist of a wisdom yet unknown to science, but his methods are 'scientific', to move from the known to the unknown, step by step, testing each before climbing to the next. The ideal for one is a star in the darkness; for the other, the carrot tied before the donkey's nose.

Meanwhile, the range of methods, means and devices is legion, and none is of more value and importance than a paper handkerchief which, when used, is flung into the fire. Each and all are fingers pointing to the moon, a favourite subject for Zen art; only the fool confuses the finger and the moon. For the means must be discarded when its use has failed, or been transcended, and it might be said that the end will not be seen until the means to it is exhausted. Buddhists are fond of the parable of the raft. A raft, sufficient to the need, is constructed at the bank of a river. It is used for the crossing, but then it is left behind. He is a fool who continues his journey to the mountain top with the raft well fastened to his back.

All devices may be used, the test of value being purely pragmatic. 'The history of Buddhist thought is marked by a bold and almost boundless experimentation with spiritual methods which were tested merely pragmatically, merely by the results attained.'[1] In an interview with the Patriarch Hui-neng a visitor was asked to set out his teacher's instruction. 'If I tell you', answered the Patriarch, 'that I have a system of Teaching to transmit to others I am cheating you. What I do to my disciples is to liberate them from their own bondage with such devices as the case may need.'[2]

All devices useful but limited

All methods and devices imply limitation. A river's breadth is bound by the banks which give it direction and power; the internal combustion engine gains its strength from the confinement of the explosion. Hence the importance of deliberately throwing away the device when its use is exhausted. All rules and habits and self-discipline are limitations, yet without them the strongest man could not proceed. A habit is excellent when used as such; how else, for example, could mind-development

[1] Edward Conze: *Buddhism*, p. 64.   [2] *The Sutra of Wei Lang*, pp. 64-5.

take place without the habit of 'right-mindfulness'? And rules are good when self-imposed or happily adopted. Indeed there are those who ask the master for actual orders on the next step to be taken, and the value of meetings is largely that those present may urge one another to do together what single-handed they might not have the energy or will to do. Yet none of these devices, whether used alone or accepted in a school or class, has greater power than that which is given it; none has authority, none is eternally 'right'. And all should be used with the only right motive, Enlightenment, and this involves the death of the self which blinds us to that state of heart and mind which is already, could we see it, within. Even here there is need for caution. As a wit has observed, the aim is not self-salvation but salvation from self.

Many a reader of this book has already made one choice, away from the Christianity of childhood to sailing bravely upon uncharted seas. Here the course set will to a large extent be psychologically determined. The pairs of opposites are strong within us, and we are all more positive or negative, more introvert or extravert, more quiet or boisterous. We all incline, for example, to the Tariki or Jiriki approach to Reality, as the Japanese say, calling on some Other Power to save us, or being content to find what we need from the Essence of Mind within. The dichotomy, as usual, is false, but it seems to be a difference. Neither alone will do for the whole of the journey, any more than the passive or active temperament will endure to the end. These divisions have long been known in the field of religion, and one of the oldest is that of the Raj Yoga of India, with its Jnana Yoga, Bhakti Yoga and Karma Yoga. The first two are the well-known pair of intellect versus emotion, with the ideal of the sage or the devotional mystic respectively. The third is of more importance for this volume, for here alone is allowance made for the man of action as I believe the typical Englishman to be. For the English criterion of worth is largely in terms of action. Tell such a man of a doctrine, and he will ask, how does it work? In a crisis he asks 'What do we do about it?', and his worst abuse of another's action is to say that 'it isn't done'. All surplus energy is passed into action, and his general restlessness is only exceeded by that of the Americans.

A trinity of method used in the West is that of science, religion and psychology. The first and last are severely limited by their definition. Science cannot be a way of life for the individual, though it may consume his total interest, and psychology has built a concrete ceiling over its head above which at present it firmly refuses to rise. In any event, psychology is concerned with the instrument of progress, with the car rather than the driver, and the Way must be trodden by a man who uses the instrument of his mind. The way of religion is a much larger subject. All religions have their genesis in the spiritual experience of a very advanced mind, and although the followers of the religion so established are working at second-hand, so to speak, they are attempting to apply what they understand of the Message which was the Master's attempt to speak of his experience. But though the way of religion is chosen by millions for its warmth and human comfort, it has its dangers for the man on the Way. As Jung pointed out in a famous passage, religion can be used as a shield to protect the individual from the very Truth which he believes he is seeking, and to many it is undoubtedly a form of escape from the problems of daily life.

The same does not apply to morality, using the word in its largest sense to include conventional ethics and all right living between man and man. But the benefits of morality are limited. It is a cleaning of the instrument rather than its use, and though it helps to create right motive and to reduce the power of self it can never do more. It does not actually lead to Enlightenment. In developing the analogy of the raft the Buddha is reported to have told his hearers, 'Ye must leave righteous ways behind, not to speak of unrighteous ways.' As Dr Suzuki points out, ethics must grow from the Enlightenment experience, and not vice versa. 'In the moral man there is a certain feeling of constraint, of giving things up which he may think properly belong to him, whereas the spiritual man moves naturally, spontaneously as flowers bloom in the spring; his mind is free from "traces" (defilements) of conflict or the choice of need.'[1] And again speaking of living by Zen as being far more than merely moral, he says, 'Morality restrains, binds; Zen releases and brings us out into a wider and freer realm of life. Morality

[1] *The Essence of Buddhism*, p. 60.

is not creative, and exhausts itself by trying to be other than itself, or rather trying to be itself.'[1]

Schools of Buddhism

There are many more 'devices' or Yanas (vehicles). The numerous schools of Buddhism alone provide a wide variety and each is right for some. Ritual has its uses, psychologically as controlling the forces of the unconscious, socially as bringing order out of the chaos of human relationship, magically as producing effects on mind and matter by a knowledge of forces not yet known to the public, and in the manifold use of symbol. There are schools of ritual gesture (Mudra Yana), and of magical sound (Mantra Yana) in Tibet, and a school involving ritual and magic passed from India to China and is now established as Shingon Buddhism in Japan. These, however, are not for the West, which makes best use of moral-philosophy as assisted by re-discoveries in the field of psychology. But the invasion of Western thought by the power of Zen has focussed attention on a choice which I believe to be, like so many others, 'falsely imagined', that between the Gradual and the Abrupt or Sudden methods of enlightenment. Historically the distinction comes from the 6th Zen Patriarch, Hui-neng (in southern dialect, Wei-lang), who was the real founder of Zen Buddhism, and taught the Sudden way to Prajna-consciousness, or Satori as it is known in Zen. His rival Shen-hsin, failing to obtain the Robe and Bowl from the 5th Patriarch, went north and, under Imperial patronage, founded the Gradual school, but it soon petered out. Is the Enlightenment which is the goal of every Buddhist attained gradually and progressively, or is it, in modern parlance, an 'existential leap' out of the relative into the Absolute? Both parties agree on a period of preparation for the great event, and the Lankavatara Sutra, one of the basic scriptures used in Zen Buddhism, talks of the purification of the mind from the defilements or 'outflows' (the analogy is to a running sore) which arises from accepting phenomena at face value. This process, it is agreed, is gradual and not instantaneous, as a potter making pots, or trees that grow up gradually. And even Zen-consciousness must, as Dr Suzuki admits, start

[1] *Living by Zen*, p. 13.

intellectually by the process of thorough negation.[1] But soon there appears a cleavage between the intellect and that Prajna-eye of the Absolute, by which alone the direct experience of Reality is obtained. How far can preparation take one to the awakening of that eye? Dr Hubert Benoit thinks no way at all. For man in fact lacks nothing, not even Enlightenment, as the Patriarch Hui-neng, already quoted, pointed out. But though the realization must be an instantaneous fusion of the two parts of the man, the normal consciousness and the Enlightenment which he has without knowing it, 'the inner work which results in the establishment of this direct contact, but not the deliverance itself, is long and difficult, and so, progressive'.[2] And later he speaks of 'the progressive elaboration of the inner conditions necessary for Satori'.[3] Agnes Arber also uses the word fusion. Speaking of the stimulus which may precede the flash of experience, she says, 'The particular moment of enlightenment may be determined by any factor which increases the intensity with which the whole man lives. The sudden flash is, in itself, of minor importance only; it is merely a signal showing that the point has been reached at which the fusion of reasoned thought and emotional consciousness comes to fulfilment in that gnosis which both outdistances and includes them. Such fusion, achieved by long effort, can give far more powerful help, in the passage from the perception of the Many to the conception of Unity, than can be gained from any fleeting ecstasy verging on delirium.'[4]

The existential leap

But once the condition is produced the actual flash or leap is 'existential'. It does not merely bring the mind just so much nearer the Truth but into and at one with the Truth. The gap is that between the relative and the Absolute, and the leap is made or it is not. As Dr Benoit says, 'In the course of his progressive preparation man brings himself nearer chronologically to his future liberty, but he does not enjoy an atom of this liberty until the moment at which he will have it in its entirety',[5]

[1] *Essays in Zen Buddhism*, Third Series, p. 202.
[2] *The Supreme Doctrine*, p. 31.
[3] Ibid., p. 219.   [4] *The Manifold and the One*, pp. 15-16.
[5] *The Supreme Doctrine*, p. 31.

and he speaks of the prisoner who files the bars of his window as never being free just a little; he is a prisoner or free. In another passage he claims that the analogy of the ladder of progress is false. Rather there is 'a road which, on the horizontal plane, runs towards the point from which the vertical axis strikes off',[1] which reminds one of Elijah being swept to heaven suddenly in a chariot of fire. Indeed I seem to remember an early speaker on Buddhism in London describing Enlightenment as stepping off the ladder of progress at right angles.

This moment is presumably the 'turning about at the seat of consciousness' which is the Buddhist moment of conversion. It is an act out of time, complete, irrevocable. It is also, as we know well, incommunicable. But surely there are degrees of Enlightenment? Dr Benoit says no. 'Either I do not see things as they are, or I see them; there is no period during which I should see little by little the Reality of the Universe.' This may be so, yet the man who 'turns about' has still a long way to go, and even an advanced Zen Master would admit that he is not yet Buddha, or anywhere near the Buddha's relation to the Absolute. For though the quality of the Enlightenment experience is incomparable with anything in the relative world, there can be more frequent and deeper moments of Enlightenment, and finally, and in the illusion of time a very long time further on, the experience is at command. Again and again we read of Zen Masters who, though delighted with the 'awakening' of the pupil, are not convinced that it is quite untainted with the relative, and press him to prove again that he can 'see'. If this may be so as to quality, is there no progress in quantity, duration and above all, the power to raise daily consciousness at will to this exalted and yet unknown plane? If so, there is another false antithesis. We need not choose the gradual or the sudden way. We are treading one and in the end will tread the other.

There are many fingers pointing to the moon which are apt to be confused with the moon. We all love authority, for it saves the fatigue of original thought, and we like to regard the Scriptures as authority. The Zen Buddhist does not do so, for one of the basic teachings of Bodhidharma was 'No depend-

[1] Ibid., p. 161.

ance upon words and scriptures.' As Hui-neng pointed out, we must not let the scriptures 'turn us round' but must learn to 'turn round' the scriptures, that is, to use the raft to cross the river and then to leave it behind. 'It is essential', said the Zen Master, Huang Po, 'not to select some particular teaching suited to a certain occasion and, being impressed by its forming part of the written canon, regard it as an inscrutable concept. Why so? Because in truth there is no immutable Dharma which the Tathagata preached.'[1] If the Dharma, the teaching of the Buddha, is not unalterable, as having no final authority as such on the mind of man, how much less can a single scripture have such authority? Better than books, as a means to the end, is companionship with the wise, for the living mind can convey what words can never enshrine. Epictetus was right. 'You must know that it is no easy thing for a principle to become a man's own unless each day he maintain it and hear it maintained.' In the absence of the great mind, the reading aloud and together of the words of the Master often carry more weight than the words read to oneself. For with a book on the knee we are apt to read as a paper is read, not savouring the meaning on or even near the plane at which the author gave his teaching utterance.

Here and now and this
And the materials for the weaving of devices? They are always here and now and this. Here, for where else could they be if we use them; now because all is Now and it is illusion to think otherwise. Of the abiding present, the 'one thought-moment' which is longer t. time, the Eternal Now in which life lives itself, there is no need to say more. Yet even at the lowest level we can but act and live and be—now; all else is the concept of the past or future, a thought which has no part in actuality. And the device or method is usable in things unholy as in things divine, in work as in play, in moments great or small, for these distinctions as all others are 'falsely imagined'. The 'this' of here and now and this is the job in hand. If I may quote again, 'The immediate work, whatever it may be, has the abstract claim of duty, and its relative importance or non-importance is not to be considered at all.' If it is right let it be done, whether

[1] *The Zen Teaching of Huang Po*, translated by John Blofeld, p. 57.

filling a pen or founding a business; if it is not right, whether founding a business or filling a pen, it is well not done. The rest is labels, slapped by the foolish onto the passing air.

The paths are many yet the Path is one. All that we know of devices are means to an end which is the beginning of the one path leading to the Goal. And the beginning is here and now and in this, this body. 'Within this very body, only six feet in length, I declare to you are the world and the origin of the world, and the ceasing of the world, and likewise the Path that leadeth to the cessation thereof.' *The Voice of the Silence*, older than this famous passage from the Anguttara Nikaya of the Pali Canon, puts it more pithily. 'Thou canst not travel on the Path before thou hast become that Path itself.' This Path awaits us all, though we shall be told of it in many languages. It has its own laws and we shall learn them. Its beginning is in a man who has largely conquered self, who 'lives but to benefit mankind', and has freed his mind from the fetters of all devices. For all these are in the end but methods, methods of enabling the individual to awaken to his own inherent Buddhahood. This being done, what matter the means that attained this end? Even the wild and senseless methods of Zen Masters become excusable. 'If there is such a thing as Zen', says Dr Suzuki, 'there must be some way in which all contradictions can be synthesized. This is where all the masters of Zen Buddhism exhaust their genius; and as they are not philosophers but pragmatists, they appeal to an experience and not to verbalism, an experience which is so fundamental as to dissolve all doubts into a harmonious unification.'[1] By this dissolution into the One are all methods seen to be such, and all abandoned. And those who abandon the raft which brought them across the river of unreality see with awakened eyes that those who came by a different raft are likewise men and women arrived at the same shore. Does it matter whence the experience, or in what guise it came?

---

[1] *Essays in Zen Buddhism*, Second series, p. 199.

Chapter 12

The Eightfold Path to Enlightenment

All that we know of Reality is the Way to it

THIS Path, described in elaborate detail in various parts of the Pali Canon, is the heart of Buddhism, for Buddhism is a Way to Enlightenment and this is the Buddha's Way. It describes the condition of mind in which the Path should be entered, the moral philosophy in which it should be trodden, and then the mental development which brings the pilgrim to the threshold of Nirvana. As this volume is dedicated to right acting rather than right action, the Path will be considered primarily from this point of view, but, as already admitted, the distinction is not easily maintained. As a Path it differs from all others save Taoism in lacking the sanction of an extra-Cosmic God. It is a system of Law without a Law-Giver, a Way of which the beginning and the end are within the mind of man. As I said in my *Buddhism*,[1] 'The Path is a system of self-development according to law, a graded process of moral evolution within the law of Karma. It is both simple and profound, simple in the clarity of its principles, profound in that its precepts rest on no external force, of God or man, but on the bedrock of immutable and natural law. It follows that the breach of any one of them is ultimately punished as unerringly as disobedience to the laws of health. The Path knows no authority save the law of which it is the manifested code, and even 'Buddhas do but point the Way'.

The whole path is within the field of rational examination and practical experiment. Nothing is taken on faith save that the Buddha has trodden such a path to its end and that the end is enormously worth while; and this may be tested and should be

[1] Pelican Series, p. 109.

tested, by practical results, at every stage. Yet, however detailed and precise, the steps are never more than principles, and whether the seeker is a king or a beggar he is offered the principles and left to work them out in his own life in his own way.

The Path is to be trodden by the whole man, and in this respect accords with the best of today's psychotherapy. From Dr Jung we know of the 'Shadow', the side of our selves we would like to forget and deny, and it is all too easy to reach to the stars with the best of us and to forget the feet which are still stuck in the clay. Man is one, however complex the parts of him, and in the eyes of the One all parts are equally untrue. Only the whole is one with the Whole, and each facet of the manifold entity used by consciousness must sooner or later be redeemed and enter Nirvana, or none at all. Nor can any part of the Path be omitted on the journey. There are no short cuts to Enlightenment. The steps may be trodden seriatim or together; the parts of the man developed as a whole or part at a time. But the whole of the Path, in this name or in that, must be trodden to the end by the whole man, and the whole of it is to be found within the compass of the human mind.

The Way is long, for though it is only from Enlightenment possessed to Enlightenment consciously known there is a long process of development before the one becomes the other. In the absence of a Saviour, each man must learn by his own error, and when he slips from the ideal Middle Way must find his way back to that razor edge and from there walk on. There will be the moment of conversion, so described in the scriptures of all the world, but this 'turning about at the seat of consciousness' is only the moment of entry on the Path proper; it may be far indeed from the goal.

The Path is a process, one end of which is in the mind of the present and the other in a distant future which will be found to be Now. As it is put in *The Sayings of the Ancient One*,[1] 'You

[1] P. G. Bowen: *The Sayings of the Ancient One*, pp. 33-38. This teaching was collected by the author from a Western-educated Atlas Berber who was content to live as the headman of a Bantu tribe. He had learnt it from scriptures written in an archaic form of Bantu no longer used. It is excellent evidence of the omnipresence of the timeless Wisdom-tradition which may be found extant in the most unexpected places.

travel an endless road, O Learner, when you walk according to the way of men, for you look back and see that it has no beginning and look forward and see that it has no end. Therefore look neither backward nor forward, but fix your eyes on each Step as you take it; then you will see that the length of the Road is only the length of the Step. Men walk the way of Time, O Child, and they mourn the Past and fear the Future. Blot out all thought of Past and Future, and suffering exists no more for you.' And again, 'Think not at all of what stature is yours. Fix no limits for your growth. It has no limits except those you create by your own willing and thinking; therefore think only of growing, and never of being full grown.' And of the steps of the Path, 'Rest upon no Step however high; if you do it will change and become a snare. Regard each step that you mount as an imperfection left behind.'

The whole man must advance upon the Way, but this must be qualified to mean the whole of the man we know at the time, who is, one might say, then in incarnation. It is obvious that if the law of Karma be true we cannot in the short span of an average life work out the effects of all past causes. We are all, as Jung has shown, predominantly more intellectual than emotional or vice versa, and more intuitive or of the senses. What, then, of the faculties not used in that life period? Jung says that, being undeveloped, they are in danger of remaining in the unconscious and there becoming worse than useless, even hostile powers, until they are given the expression which is their right. To become whole, to rob those powers of evil, we must descend into the darkness of our own minds and, in the light of consciousness, recognize and learn to use these karmic debts. But this implies the assistance of an expert, or a most exceptional mind. Most of us must accept ourselves as the product of but part of our own past actions, with much more, like the proverbial iceberg, unseen and as yet unknown. Meanwhile, the task in hand is to destroy the self as it rears its head unceasingly, to ennoble the Self which moves from life to life until this, too, is 'dropped' or made one with the infinite, and so move steadily to the goal which, at present but an ideal concept, has yet to be made real by pure experience.

Lily Abegg, author of a truly bridge-building volume, *The*

Mind of East Asia, points out to East and West the difference in their several approaches to Reality. The East, she says, has always been aware of the unconscious, and handled it as either friend or foe, on the higher levels coming to terms with it by what the West calls individuation, and on the lower levels admitting a host of gods and spirits who must be either governed or coerced by magic of many kinds. For those of the East the 'total' view is easy, and they approach all problems, including that of self-development from a dozen points at once, pragmatic, intuitive, psychological and magical, but never confined to the logical straight-line technique of the West. If the path of progress be regarded as spiral, the East moves smoothly up the incline; the West moves vertically, and notices the violent effort needed to achieve each 'step' between the coils. For the West, the ladder; for the East, 'grow as the flower grows'. If the Western virility is offset by the tolerance, humility and patience of the East, here is but another of the sets of opposites, between which lies the Middle Way that few of us yet tread. Both are agreed, however, that the treading of the Path is a matter for every plane. On the physical, the gravely neglected psychic, the emotional, the lower and higher planes of mind, on all these must the Path be trodden, and its final stages bring the wakening of the 'Thousand-petalled Lotus' by the sunlight of an intuition roused, developed and brought under the will. Whether the ladder be viewed from above or below it is a process of return to the One, and the sanction for obedience to the commands inseverable from the Path is therefore from the top. None drives us to move upward; there is a pull from the One, the light of home to which the prodigal son, however tardily, returns.

Morality and Enlightenment

Here, then, is another reason why morality alone is not enough for 'salvation', if by morality is meant no more than pure living and noble thinking. Yet the link is close. As Aldous Huxley says, 'The relationship between moral action and spiritual knowledge is circular, as it were, and reciprocal. Selfless behaviour makes possible an accession of knowledge, and the accession of knowledge makes possible the performance of further and more genuinely selfless actions, which in their turn enhance the agent's capacity for knowing.'[1] Thus the Self, within my definition, is progressively prepared for the 'moment', the 'turning about at the seat of consciousness' which is conversion to new values and new (intuitive) vision of Reality. In this moment of the second birth the Self is 'saved' from illusion, the doctrine of Anatta (no permanent self) is made true by experience, and consciousness is free to surrender itself as such before the mystery, in its purest sense, of Nirvana.

Four Noble Truths

Meanwhile the urge of the Path, the pressure to move forward and upward, is the release from suffering. Of the Four Noble Truths of Buddhism, the first is the omnipresence of suffering, which characterizes all phenomena. The second Noble Truth is that the cause of most of our suffering is desire, the desire of self for its selfish gratification. The third Truth is that that which has been caused can be removed by the removal of the cause. The Fourth Truth is the Noble Eightfold Path which, by removing the cause of the suffering, the self and its desires, removes and puts an end to suffering. The purpose of the Path is, then, precise, to break the circle of desire and suffering. At what particular point the circle is broken is immaterial, and in the elaboration of the cycle of inter-related causation, the Buddhist 'Wheel of Life', it is pointed out that if any sequence is broken the 'man', however defined, is free. All this has value for our purpose as providing the necessary impetus or motive power for beginning to tread the Path. The right motive for its continuance is one of its steps, and can be considered later.

The Path is the Buddha's Middle Way, and must be so. If all is One, then all the pairs of opposites are 'falsely imagined', and only the ideal Middle Way contains that non-existent moment between past and future which is the Now, that point in space which is nowhere but Here, and that fusion of contradictories which, being action in the light of Prajna, alone is karmaless and 'right'. Negatively directed to the end of suffering, positively to the achievement of Samadhi as a prelude to Nirvana, the Path is an attack on self in the interests of Self,

[1] *The Perennial Philosophy*, p. 129.

and on Self in order that even this expedient notion may in turn die out before the light of Enlightenment. As Aldous Huxley pithily puts it, ' "Our Kingdom go" is the necessary and unavoidable corollary of "Thy Kingdom come". For the more there is of self the less there is of God.'[1]

The Eightfold Path is the heart of the Theravada school of Buddhism, and belongs, therefore, to the realm of moral-philosophy rather than metaphysics. In the Mahayana, the eightfold analysis gives way to six Paramitas, or transcendental virtues, but both formulations are elaborations of a basic trinity of development consisting of Sila, which covers morality, Samadhi, which covers the field of mental development by meditation, and Prajna, the supernal Wisdom which pertains to the Absolute, or as near to it as the human mind can gain. The importance of any such classification is not its detail but the fact that it is inclusive and complete. No more is needed, no Saviour, no extra-cosmic Law, no faith save in the scientist's sense of the provisional acceptance of a working hypothesis. The rest is a matter of right action, of actually treading the Way.

The Eightfold Path

Of the Eightfold analysis, the first step is Right Views, or a correct mental attitude to the subject. In Buddhist terms this is a right point of view which includes dropping (the binding element in) all specific views. The Theravadin would mention the Three Signs of Being, the Four Noble Truths, with Kamma and Rebirth and some understanding, albeit negative, of Nirvana (in Pali, Nibbana). The Zen student would say of the first step that it should never have been included, in that all views are a hindrance on the Way, but the Middle Way might satisfy both Schools in that all views are provisional, and so long as they are seen as so many means or devices they may be used and will not be abused. Certainly, some mental preparation is advisable at the outset of the journey, for how shall the climb begin without 'views' on the suffering of life about one, the difference at the top, the purpose and motive of the climb, and the mechanism, so to speak, of movement? At least the omnipresence of change, born of the fundamental unreality of all

[1] Ibid, p. 113.

phenomena, must be well in mind, for he who is content with a house will not leave it. Only when it is seen that the house of self is burning with the fires of hatred, lust and illusion is an urge born to abandon it, and the Way is a method of letting the fires die for want of fuelling.

The second step involves right motive, which is not the same as purpose. The purpose of the Path may be Enlightenment, but why does the pilgrim seek Enlightenment? So long as the reward of climbing is sought for self there will be further sorrow. 'Not to seek for anything, O Bhikkhus, is to be free; to seek for anything is not to be free.'[1] In my own *Buddhism* I analysed motive as acting on three planes. 'The sanction of Buddhist morality is threefold. At its lowest it is purely selfish. An understanding of the law of Karma makes one realize that it "pays" to be good. This is the sanction of all man-made laws, and the Buddhist knows that the moral laws of nature carry with them both the punishment of disobedience and the virtuous man's reward. In Buddhism a man is punished by his sins, not for them. Later comes the rational basis of morality. If life be one, each unit of that life reacts in all it does for good or evil on each other unit of the whole. Hence to do evil is to harm one's fellow men, while the strict morality of one such unit raises the level of all humanity. Finally comes the ideal stage of motiveless morality, a realization that the highest virtue is in truth its own reward.' At this stage the advice of the *Bhaga-vad Gita*[2] becomes operative. 'Let the motive for action be in the action itself, not in the event', but if the two be separated, the motive is more important than the act. The power of thought is far greater than any force on the physical plane, for it is by past thinking that we are what we are. If the motive is right, the wrong of an act in error may be swiftly purged; if the motive be selfish, the deed itself, however good, is tainted by that error, with all its consequences.

So much for the preliminaries of the Path, right basic principles about phenomena and the laws which rule the universe, and right motive for entering it at all. The next three steps concern right ethics or morality, but if the order is not fortuitous it is interesting. Right Speech precedes right Action and

---

[1] *Samyutta Nikaya*, XXII 35.   [2] From pp. 108-9.

this in turn precedes right Livelihood. Sound, in the esoteric tradition, is of immense power, and in the Indian science of Yoga there is a school of Mantra Yoga, or the right use of phrases pitched to a secret wave-length or vibration. In the beginning, as is stated in the Gospel of St John, was the Word. This being so, all schools of self-development stress the value of silence, negative lest sound be abused, positive in that silence contains thought-power inturned to subjective uses. As Polonius counsels his son Laertes on going overseas—'Give thy thoughts no tongue, nor any unproportioned thought his act.' If we should think before acting, that the act may be right, we should think before speaking, itself a powerful form of action for good or ill. For thought moves on its own plane, and thoughts indeed are things. A thought of evil can wound as healing thoughts can heal, and each brings its own reaction. Hence the grave evil of gossip, the cause of which is invariably ill-will, from spite or jealousy or fear, and to the student of right acting a powerful hindrance to any progress on the Way. Right Action, the fourth step is covered by the term Sila which, as already stated, is the second of the trinity of progress from what we are to what we would be. As it deals with what should be done rather than with the right doing of it no more need be said than what I wrote in my *Walk On!*, 'The term morality includes at least two separate though related parts, ethics and character-building. The former concerns our relations with our fellow men; the latter, the purification of character and the extinction of the three fires of hatred, lust and illusion which in most of us burn so merrily. It has never been put more pithily than in the *Dhammapada*. "Irrigators guide water; fletchers straighten arrows; carpenters bend wood; wise men shape themselves."'[1] Of these two the introverted activity of mind control and development is highly relevant to right acting, and will be further considered in the next chapter. Right Livelihood is an extrovert activity, and should, of course, be in keeping with the highest ideals of ethics, in the world of today no easy matter.

The sixth step, Right Effort, is once more an attitude of mind, and of some importance to this thesis. The right direction of

[1] p. 63.

the effort is set out in any textbook of Buddhism; here we are concerned with the nature of the effort rather than its proper direction. It must be commensurate with the total situation, including the powers of the user and the state of his circumstance. Too much effort, all the more so if suddenly applied in a burst of enthusiasm, will merely produce an equal and opposite reaction; too little, being laziness masked as something better, will delay the achievement of right acting. The middle way is subtle and not easy to find. As Floyd Ross wrote, 'Right effort involves many things—the control of the passions, avoidance of evil thoughts, stimulation of right states of mind. In this all important discipline there is apparently a "right velocity" at which one should travel. This fine point of balance between undue striving and undue laxity might be symbolized by the tuning of a delicate stringed instrument.'[1] And there must of course be periods of relaxation after those of highest tension, when the instrument, to pursue the analogy, is unstrung, a fact which enthusiasts in right action or right meditation are apt to forget. Discipline there must be, and self-discipline at that, but the discipline itself must be right for the occasion or it will not set the mind and hence the actor free.

Mind-development

So much for Sila, morality in its widest sense, but this, as already pointed out, will not in itself go far. Then comes Bhavana, mental development, and from the Buddhist point of view this is perhaps the real entrance to the Path. There is an interesting section in the *Dhammapada* which reads, 'Let a man guard his speech, train his mind and do no evil with his body. Then let him enter the Path.' But if the training of the mind be the seventh and eighth steps on the Path then the entrance to the Path is at the close of the final step of Samadhi, and it is interesting that this final step is Samadhi, and not Nirvana itself. For Samadhi is far from the Goal, and it may be that the Eightfold Path is an expanded version of the famous passage from the same scripture, 'Cease to do evil; learn to do good; cleanse your own heart; this is the teaching of the Buddhas.' Perhaps it is only then that the final Path is entered, and there may be

[1] *The Meaning of Life in Hinduism and Buddhism*, p. 112.

many ways for reaching its entrance. But of the final Path, on which new rules apply that are not lightly written, the Buddha was adamant, that any teaching which did not include it was not 'right'. Meanwhile, with the six steps safely trodden the pilgrim is faced for the first time with his own mind, and the need to conquer it. From now on the Way is mystical, within. 'Thou canst not travel on the Path before thou has become that Path itself', says *The Voice of the Silence*, and the mystics of the world make echo. Henceforth the subject of attention is the self, and the Self, and the SELF, if the pilgrim can ascend so far, till the Many is again the One and even the One returned to whence it came.

Chapter 13

Mind-Development

Our Essence of Mind is intrinsically pure; all things are only its manifestations, and good deeds and evil deeds are only the result of good thoughts and evil thoughts respectively.

THE SUTRA OF WEI LANG

All that we are is the result of what we have thought; it is founded on our thoughts, made up of our thoughts.

DHAMMAPADA

RIGHT acting is of course controlled by the mind, and the foregoing chapters of this work are so many preludes to consideration of its nature and development. The Path which all men sooner or later tread with full deliberation is that from Enlightenment possessed but yet unknown to Enlightenment in fullest consciousness. At the beginning of the Path we need, as already conceded, a body of concepts or 'views' as the raw material of experiment. Then we must learn right action in order to cleanse the vehicles through which we gain and express experience, and to rectify past Karma and its consequences. Then, having 'ceased to do evil' and 'learned to do good', we must 'cleanse our own hearts' in a long and weary process of mind-expansion from the realm of thought to that of No-thought, from knowledge 'about' to consciousness of Reality.

The metaphysical basis of mind-development is the postulate of Mind-only, that from the Absolute comes the One which is the One-Mind, and from the One the many. It is in this world of duality, where the discriminating consciousness of every day life holds sway, that we must prepare the approach to Prajna-consciousness, that super-awareness of Non-duality which is the heart of Enlightenment, and therefore the goal of all man's efforts in the field of mind. Along this Path there is no smooth progress to the Goal. As already explained, there is no existent bridge between relative and absolute, and when the best instrument of the relative, the thinking mind, has reached its limit there is a moment without precedent in many a life of self-preparation for Enlightenment. The whole force of will, developed and trained in the hard field of competition, harnessed now to a motive purged of self, and driving an intellect developed to its last degree, must come to the edge of the precipice beyond which thought can go no further, and then—jump. Only this existential leap, irrational, nonsensical, can waken consciousness beyond its limits of duality; nothing less will waken the Prajna-eye which sees the One and the Many in a single glance beyond all difference.

This is a tremendous and ultimate process. All men seek it, in this name or that, and all use a number of technical terms which may be of help in that particular school but hinder the students of another. Here, no more will be used than may seem necessary to express quite differing points of view and, what is more important, ways of mind-development. For the mind is complex, and for these purposes includes the psychic plane above the physical, the emotions, the work-a-day mind of discrimination, the more abstract mind of synthetic thought, the intuition as known to Western psychology, and that Prajna-intuit'on, as Dr Suzuki calls it, which is not the intuitive awareness of anything, as there has ceased to be anything separate of which the intuition may be aware.

In *Concentration and Meditation*, devised by the Buddhist Society, London as a textbook for Buddhists in the West in the days when there was little else available, a division of the subject was made into Concentration, Lower and Higher Meditation, and Contemplation. The analysis is arbitrary, and other schools in all parts of the world use different methods of division. All that matters is that certain practical distinctions be kept clear in mind, and one is that between concentration and meditation. As was said in the book of that name, 'Until the mind has been thoroughly and patiently trained in concentration it is both useless and dangerous to attempt to meditate, useless because the student will lack the faculty of one-pointed thought which is essential to successful meditation, dangerous because the application of uncontrolled and untrained energies to spiritual problems will all too easily result in moral and mental disturbances, reacting through bodily disorders on the physical plane.'[1]

Concentration

On the subject of concentration there are many handy volumes; here it need only be mentioned to distinguish it from mind-development. As I wrote in *Walk On!*, 'Before a man can fence he must learn to handle a rapier, so that rapier, hand and eye can follow the will as one; before a girl can dance she must train her muscles till the body as a whole will express the beauty in the mind; before a man can use his mind to develop his inner faculties, to increase his understanding and to integrate the vast range of related principles and parts which make up "self", he must develop and learn to control and use the needful instrument.'[2] A sound analogy is the searchlight. A precision instrument, it is an efficient and impersonal machine. It can be directed at will, moved rapidly from object to object, focussed as needed and at will turned off. The source of power is electricity, which no man has ever seen save in its results on matter so-called, and this power is inexhaustible.

But concentration is not in the least 'spiritual', and the most material-minded person uses it every day. We concentrate on the job in hand, or we do not do it effectively, and to some extent the object of concentration is under the direction of the will. But this interest, which is the object of concentration, is generally determined as it were, from outside; it is a reaction to emotional interest, or the pull of 'duty' in that it is the next thing which in the circumstances must be done. Other attractions are in the meantime kept at bay by the pressure of attention on the object which at the moment holds the field. But in these conditions, how easily is the mind distracted, that is, drawn elsewhere to another object. How few of us can concentrate on a difficult letter while the telephone rings, the doorbell

[1] Christmas Humphreys: *Concentration and Meditation*, 1935, pp. 80-1.
[2] *Walk On!*, pp. 38-9.

rings, a voice talks on the radio, two people talk in the room, and all the while one is wondering whether or not to go to the dentist with a bad toothache?

True concentration begins when the object chosen is determined beforehand by the will without reference to interest or to like or dislike. It is instructive to note the reaction of a class of students to the suggestion that, timed by a friend, they should attempt to concentrate for five minutes on the door-knob, without allowing any other object or thought to arise. True, it is 'useless', but either one can do it or one can not. If one cannot, is it right to speak of a mind yet ready for that 'unwavering steadiness of heart upon the arrival of every event whether favourable or unfavourable' of which the *Bhagavad Gita* speaks? 'Wherever the eye looks, the heart is directed also', says *The Secret of the Golden Flower*. Have we learnt to control the eye, or at least our reaction to what it sees? 'But when you fix your heart at one point', says the same work, 'then nothing is impossible to you.' Even the Indian science of Yoga is no more. 'Concentration or Yoga', runs the second verse of the *Yoga Aphorisms* of Patanjali, 'is the hindrance of the modifications of the thinking principle', that is, control of the thoughts.

But though the rider of the stallion may fancy himself on the animal's back, the stallion strongly objects to all attempt at control. The result is like a Wild West Rodeo but it goes on longer. Nor is the animal completely broken to the rider's will until the intellect is integrated with the intuition, and both with an awareness of their non-duality as seen with a Prajna-eye. Students cannot understand why concentration is said to be difficult when in a sense they are using it every day. The reason is that the object chosen deliberately has no attraction to the mind; it does not like it, does not want it, and gets no 'kick' of interest out of it. Hence concentration is easy on a symphony, a travel book or the writing of this chapter; but how different is the door-knob, without interest, profit or any form of appeal.

Looking at things
One exercise in concentration used by Buddhists is just to look at things. The artist learns to look at a tree, a face or a vase of

flowers. The philosopher takes this into the realm of meaning or significance. He notices how each 'thing' is in a state of flux, perpetually changing. If a student of the Mahayana school he will look for the 'suchness' (Tathata) of each thing and see that suchness as essentially empty or void (sunya) of all predicates or attributes, being merely a brief phenomenon 'falsely imagined' by the ignorance-laden mind. He will go further, and appreciate that all he sees is 'right', whether or not he likes it, or approves of it. This involves profound concentration on each 'thing' experienced, to see what it is, what it means. But the viewing must be objective and remain so. Says the *Dhammapada*, 'As rain breaks into an ill-thatched house so craving breaks into an ill-trained mind.' There must be concentration without entanglement, and this by control of reaction. With reaction under control the object may be enjoyed to the full, as a man may enjoy a cigar who can easily give up smoking, or wealth if he is not bound by it. Even when the Prajna-eye of non-duality is opened, 'it does not teach to destroy the impulses, instincts and affective factors that make up the human heart; it only teaches to clear our intellectual insight from erroneous discriminations and unjustifiable assertions; for when this is done the heart knows by itself how to work out its native virtues'.[1]

This is the science of 'right recollectedness' as taught by Buddhism, and often misunderstood. Its purpose is to bring thought under control by having clear and objective awareness of every act and moment in the period of the exercise. Thus walking, taken for granted, is analysed aloud into every movement. 'There is a raising of the right foot, of the right knee, of the hip. There is a setting down of the right foot . . .' The idea is that a mind so aware of its actions and surroundings can apply this awareness to the logical, impersonal use of the finest dialectic for the analysis of each thought-process, and thence to the ultimate processes of all phenomena. A mind so trained is not thereby more 'spiritual', but it becomes a beautiful instrument under the control of its user; it can be used for all that pertains to thinking and, as the Zen Buddhist would say, for

[1] Suzuki: *Studies in the Lankavatara Sutra*, p. 101.

reaching the limits of thought with a view to passing beyond them.

Concentration, then, is the creation of the instrument; meditation is the use of it. 'Concentration involves contraction of the field of vision, but meditation involves its expansion. In concentration we gain clear vision, in meditation we keep that clear vision but extend it over a larger field and into depths and heights of thought which we have not been able to reach clearly before.'[1]

Meditation

But the whole process of meditation is inturned. It may be 'with seed' or 'without seed', but the seed or object is itself an idea or concept, and the whole process is aimed at enlarging the field of consciousness with more and more of the Essence of Mind which, in a thousand names, is the whole of which the mind we know is such a small and ill-lit part. 'To meditate', said Hui-neng, 'means to realize inwardly the imperturbability of the Essence of Mind.' For 'Our Essence of Mind is intrinsically pure; all things are only its manifestations, and good deeds and evil deeds are only the result of good thoughts and evil thoughts respectively.' Hence the constant effort by a score of means to achieve an inner balance, the Silence, the Darkness (from which came the Light), the Universal as distinct from our painfully human mind. This is the process of cleansing the mind of discrimination, of dropping the foolish beliefs of difference, of ideas which act as stumbling blocks to the flow of life. Yet when all are dropped there is no emptiness of mind, for nature abhors a vacuum in thought as in all else. This still extant belief, that there is virtue in emptying the mind, was stamped upon by Hui-neng in the eighth century. 'Common people attach themselves to objects without; and within, they fall into the wrong idea of "vacuity". When they are able to free themselves from attachment to objects when in contact with objects, and from the fallacious view of annihilation on the doctrine of the "void" they will be free from delusions within and from illusions without.' Sunyata, the Void, is very different, for this, the ultimate understanding of the 'no-soul' theory of the

[1] Ernest Wood: *Concentration*, p. 93.

Theravada school, is Absolute, and being an absolute void is also absolute fullness. Here is no emptiness, as an absence of things, but an absence of all distinctions between things or thoughts or any knots in the ceaseless flow of becoming. Sunya is seen when all stoppage of the flow of life is ended. Only when thought flows without hindrance is there No-thought, with no stop or blocking between awareness and expression. Thus to transfer the attention when it is caught by an outside object is to block the transmission of power as chosen. In terms of swordsmanship, as Zen Masters frequently point out, the man who pauses to think between decision and blow is probably a dead man, for his opponent will have struck 'without thinking'.

The goal of meditation, then, whatever the method used, is a steady withdrawal of energy from the periphery of consciousness to that 'still centre of the turning world' wherein alone is found that 'transparent luminosity of thought' which is in fact No-thought. Such thought is described as 'thought which is neither conjoined with passion, nor disjoined from it; which is neither conjoined with nor disjoined from hate, confusion, obsessions, coverings, unwholesome tendencies, fetters or what makes for views. That is the transparent luminosity of thought.'[1] In such a condition, however rarely achieved or shortly held, the 'suchness' of each apparently separate 'thing' is seen as 'void' yet absolute to that thing, and in this sense one with all other things in an 'unimpeded interdiffusion', as described in the difficult teaching of Jijimuge of the Kegon school of Japanese Buddhism. This world of suchness is void of particulars because, in Alan Watts' fine phrase, 'it teases the mind out of thought, dumbfounding the chatter of definition so that there is nothing left to be said'.[2] Yet such a man is not out of the world. He is in the world yet not of it, and he strives to unite the apparent distinction by a process of perpetual mindfulness. This effort to be 'mindful and self-possessed' should hold a large part of the day's attention. How is it done? In the Digha Nikaya of the Pali Canon the Buddha describes it as follows. 'A Bhikkhu in his going forth and in his home-returning acts composedly. In looking forward and in looking back he acts composedly.

[1] Edward Conze: *Selected Sayings from the Perfection of Wisdom*, p. 104.
[2] *The Way of Zen*, p. 131.

In wearing his robes and bearing his bowl; in eating, drinking, chewing, swallowing; in relieving nature's needs; in going, standing, sitting, sleeping, waking, speaking, keeping silence, he acts composedly. That, O Bhikkhus, is how a Bhikkhu is self-possessed.' And he is 'mindful' in the perpetual awareness that the so-called self is a compound, having no unchanging and immortal part or principle which separates it from the whole.

'Mindful and Self-possessed'

In the opinion of Dr A. Coomaraswamy, the importance of being 'mindful and self-possessed' in the least of our daily actions can hardly be exaggerated. 'The Buddhist emphasis on mindfulness can hardly be exaggerated; nothing is to be done absent-mindedly or with respect to which one could say "I did not mean to do it"; an inadvertent sin is worse than a deliberate sin.' The doctrine is not new to the West. As the same writer makes clear, Plato taught much the same. 'Do nothing but in accordance with the leading of the immanent Principle, nothing against the Common Law that rules the whole body, never yielding to the pulls of the affections, whether for good or evil; this is what Self-mastery means.'[1] From the view-point of right acting the importance of the doctrine is that it works all the time. It thus destroys the distinction of holy and profane, of important and unimportant, of worldly and spiritual. Dr Suzuki quotes a traditional story about Hojo Tokimune, who saved Japan from the Mongol invasions in the thirteenth century. Tokimune visited Bukko, a famous Teacher of his day, and asked his advice about cowardice. He was told to throw away his thoughts of Tokimune, in whom alone any thoughts of cowardice could find their source. When he asked how to throw away his cherished self he was told, 'Shut out your thoughts.' 'How can I shut out all my thoughts from consciousness?' asked Tokimune. 'Sit cross-legged in meditation', said the Master, 'and see into the source of all your thoughts which you imagine as belonging to Tokimune.' Said Tokimune, 'I have so much of worldly affairs to look after, and it is difficult to find spare moments for meditation.' The answer may be applied to all of us. 'Whatever worldly affairs you are engaged

[1] *Hinduism and Buddhism*, pp. 56-7.

in, take them up as occasions for your inner reflection, and some day you will find out who is this beloved Tokimune of yours.'[1]

Once the habit of meditation is achieved, not merely as a daily exercise in the mind's withdrawal from the margin of consciousness, but as the mental stance, so to speak, in which to face all circumstance, it is a matter of time before the results are seen in circumstance, and what is more important, in the mind's reaction to that circumstance. Then is it seen to be true, in the words of the first verse of the *Dhammapada*, that 'All that we are is the result of what we have thought; it is founded on our thoughts and made up of our thoughts.' As we think so we become; as we have thought so we are. Right causes, therefore, are more important than thoughts of right effects, for if the cause is right the effect will be right, and it is the former alone that is under our immediate control.

Meditation, then, is the right use of the mind, as prepared by exercises in concentration, to control the movement of consciousness. In most of us it is at the mercy of outside stimulus, by sight or sound, or of internal stimulus by the bubbling up of thought under the impetus of past action, but as more and more it comes under the control of the will it may be used precisely as decided and not otherwise.

Methods of meditation
Of the technique of meditation little need here be said. The schools and methods vary enormously, with temperament, immediate purpose and the stage of evolution of the practitioner. Much will depend on the level, as it were, at which it is to be practised, ranging from the 'character-building' which works at emotional-intellectual level to build in needed virtues and to eliminate faults, to pure contemplation, which is the province of the great mystics in all periods and all parts of the earth. Even the nature of the 'centre in the midst of conditions', as it is called in *The Secret of the Golden Flower*, will vary, from a mere concept of unity to an actual awareness, in a timeless 'thought-moment', of that centre which is nowhere, in a circle that has no circumference. But whether the exercise in formal meditation be taken from Indian Yoga or the Theravada scriptures of

[1] From *Zen Buddhism and its Influence on Japanese Culture*, p. 40.

Buddhism, or from the Golden Flower of Chinese practice, certain distinctions apply, and one is that between the psychic and the spiritual. The mind, as already seen, is enormously complex, and from the plane just above the physical, the psychic or 'astral' realm, the abode of 'ghosts', elementals, and forces good and evil of all kinds, to that serene level of selfless awareness which we vaguely call spiritual, is a far cry, and a long journey for the pilgrim who seeks Reality. *The Voice of the Silence* has much to say of the dangers of the psychic plane— and a large majority of us are at least slightly psychic—and in the absence of competent training it is easy to mistake the glamour of an awakening psychic awareness for the genuine 'experience' of spiritual vision. There are tests whereby to know the difference. The one brings pride in achievement, even a boastfulness of 'powers' not yet possessed by the many, and the teacher who makes such a boast, or takes one penny for his teaching is not on the Path which leads to Nirvana. This is of the self, earthy, and binds the pilgrim in new fetters as he slowly sheds the old. The experience of 'trances', visions of light and colour, periods of lightness of body and the like, have little relation to the awakening of Prajna, that im-mediate, direct awareness of Reality.

The detail of meditation is set out in a score of volumes, and is well described in a manuscript dating from the Sung Dynasty of China.[1] Here there is but space to quote the ending. 'After the rising (from the meditation seat) let him always contrive to retain whatever mental power he has gained by meditation, as if he were watching over a baby; for this will help him in maturing the power of concentration.' This picture of hourly watching over the baby of a new-born power is delightful. Certainly, to change the analogy, the new plant will die unless cared for, and tended day by day.

The subject will vary with the school, the particular teacher, or the needs of the pupil or practitioner. It is unimportant, and is but a means or 'device', a finger pointing to the moon. What matters is not the subject but the power gained by using it, the development thereby acquired. In any event the subject in the end is one and the same, the triple subject of the self, the

[1] See Dr Suzuki's *Essays in Zen Buddhism*, Second Series, pp. 284-7.

Self and the SELF. The self must be destroyed for ever. It is illusion and an illusion that is the cause of suffering. The Self is also a changing entity, but the worst of it is steadily 'dropped' as the best of it is slowly developed. In the end, in Satori, or whatever one calls the moment of Enlightenment, this Self is face to face with its own totality, and sees its face before Heaven and Earth were born. It is this brief vision of the Original Face, as it is called in Zen Buddhism, that makes it easier to assume the best in others and the worst in oneself. The first makes for greater charity; the second for greater humility.

In time comes the moment of 'conversion', of a vision of things as they are so that nothing is ever the same hereafter. The One is known as the One, and THAT which lies beyond is perceived as possible; the Many is seen as the One in another form. Thereafter, in 'contemplation', of which nothing can be usefully written, the mind is made free from fetters. Only 'the Mind that alights nowhere' is free to know All-Mind, but the meditator will not reach this high condition until there has developed in him, in the meditation hour and in daily use, a faculty that will replace the intellect as dominant, that *knows* as distinct from knowing *about*, that is not bound by the limitations of dual thought and its conceptual machinery, for it sees in a world of non-duality, and knows as the intellect can never know. This is the intuition, whose higher ranges reach to that special form of it which Dr Suzuki calls Prajna-intuition. This faculty, the sole means whereby the mind may know Reality, is for many a new instrument. Let us examine it.

Chapter 14

From Intellect to Intuition

Do not follow in the footsteps of the ancients;
seek what they sought.   BASHO

THE Self, however spelt, is immensely complex, far more so than most Western investigators would have us believe. But most psychologists, and these are more concerned than any with the ingredients of the mind, agree that it contains at least four 'planes' or faculties or functions. The first is sensation, pertaining to the five senses and their message to the brain; the second is what most call the emotions, but which psychology now calls affects; the third is thought, the product of the intellect, which we are here considering, and the fourth is the intuition, as distinct in its nature and functioning from the others as they from each other. Beyond these four lies Atman, say the sages of the East, the 'Spirit' of St Paul, but it is not the property of any man, for all that we know of man is Anatta as the Theravadin Buddhists say, having no Atta (Atman) or spiritual self-principle which eternally distinguishes that entity from any other.

Of these four functions the highest and lowest, using the analogy of a lighthouse for the Self as a whole, are alone direct sources of knowledge. All sensuous experience is direct, in that no other process intervenes, for example, between a hand that falls on something very hot and the resulting message to the brain. In the same way the intuition, or Buddhi as the East knows it, the faculty of Bodhi or Prajna, Wisdom, though undeveloped in most of us, and as yet beyond our control is, when it speaks, direct, complete and unmistakable as a flash of lightning on a dark night. It is also, in its message of Reality, incommunicable in terms of thought or emotion.

The nature of the emotions so far eludes the Western psychologist. For Jung it is synonymous with 'affect' which he called in *Psychological Types*, 'a state of feeling characterized by a perceptible bodily innervation on the one hand and a peculiar disturbance of the ideational process on the other' (p. 522). Whence it springs is still, it would seem, unknown. Whether it is a function of the mind in the larger sense, or periodic intrusions from the unconscious does not seem to be clear, but that its criterion of values is like and dislike, as distinct from true and untrue, is accepted. Here, it is sufficient to say that the emotions stand, as Jung equates them, at one end of the bi-polar field of the mind at the other of which stands the intellect. And like the thoughts of the intellect, the emotions are always reactions to outside stimuli, as with fear or love or hate, and never a means of direct experience.

The Intellect
The intellect, the thought-machine which digests and evaluates experience according to its own requirements, is always indirect, and the finest intellect never knows more than *about* the object of enquiry. Its food is sensation from below and intuitive experience from above, but it also feeds on thought-material already acquired, or newly acquired second-hand, as the thoughts of others.

Jung, soon after giving the world his type-analysis of the Introvert and Extravert, offered his four functions in two pairs of the Intellect/Feelings and the Intuitive/Sensational. This analysis, mentioned in Chapter Two, is now well known, but for those in search of fresh examination it is well set out in the first chapter of Dr Jacobi's *The Psychology of C. G. Jung*. Dr Jung points out that all of us have these four faculties but that in none of us are they equally developed. Always one of each pair is better developed than the other, and the latter, being 'inferior', remains as to part undifferentiated, while the part in consciousness is apt to be repressed and thrust back into the unconscious, whence it escapes in devious and embarrassing forms in an attempt to restore the lost equilibrium. As he has recently written, 'the discrepancy between intellect and feeling, which get in each other's way at the best of times, is a particularly painful chapter in the history of the human psyche'.[1] All who have trained the intellect to a precision instrument know how fatal to accuracy is any irruption of the emotions, and how a decision which should turn on hard thinking may be wrongly given when personal feeling, one way or the other, enters in. Let us then look at the intellect, this instrument of thought which must be fully developed and then by the development of a higher faculty, transcended.

It is essentially a thought-machine, a magnificent means for arriving at the finest awareness of Reality short of its direct experience. It exists in each of us, and may be and ultimately will be developed to perfection in all. It would seem that we are, in the long road of evolution, at the point when Manas, mind, is the faculty to be developed, and the very word *man* is derived from *manas* which in turn is derived from the root to think. As a faculty in control of the will it is more rare than the average man will admit. Few who glibly say on all occasions and about all subjects, 'I think', are in fact yet able to do so. Most are but reflecting, parrot-like, the opinions but half understood of others; the original thinker is remarkably rare.

The intellect has a wide range of power. It can analyse and synthesize, criticize and compare. It can accept or reject a concept, or from others create a blend which as such is new. By increasingly accurate and patient use it can learn more and more about all phenomena, including the human mind. But great though its power may become it has limitations which may be clearly defined. In particular, though it may know *about* it, it can never know, in the sense that I know pain when I put my hand in the fire. Its knowledge must ever be incomplete and to that extent inaccurate, for it will always be composed of a synthesis of items of information as distinct from that im-mediate identity of knower and known which is the prerogative of a faculty of knowledge beyond the reach and range of the intellect.

The machinery of thought lays down, as it were, its own tramlines and runs on them. The rules of logic are artificial, but logic is a mode of using concepts to arrive at the desired result. The East shares with the West the use of dialectic, but

[1] *The Undiscovered Self*, p. 94.

rather for destroying the bonds of thought than for arriving at an intellectual solution of a super-intellectual problem. As Lily Abegg points out in her *Mind of East Asia*, the Eastern approach to spiritual truth is very different from the tram-line approach of the West, for whereas logic and other mental processes may 'prove' a proposition to the satisfaction of the thinking machine, not thus can the essential truth of Reality ever be proved to the satisfaction of the Spiritual faculties. The mind may reason; the heart, in Hui-neng's sense of the Essence of Mind, knows, and it does not thus know by the intellect.

Thoughts are things

The intellectual unit is the concept or thought-form, and thoughts are as much things as the bricks with which a house is built. Life and form are the 'opposites' of which each 'thing' is constructed, and a thought consists of some portion of the universal life clothed in material which, though invisible, is none the less malleable on its own plane. Thus a thought can be projected into the mental atmosphere and have its effect, and a thought charged with emotion is visible to the psychic. Nearly all our knowledge is in the form of concepts, including memory and anticipation; and all thought-processes whether of philosophy or mathematics, composing music or writing, and all forms of formal communication are the manipulation of thought-forms old or new. All theories of the universe are here included, and for most of us the very term God. Few indeed are they who can say that they know beyond the level of concept. These are the mystics, the poets and others with the intuition well developed. The rest of us know about, though we may know a great deal about, and in a world of specialized knowledge the old joke is becoming true, that a specialist is a man who learns more and more about less and less.

Above all we are at the mercy of concepts for the communication of ideas and experience of all kinds, including that direct experience of Reality which can never in fact be communicated, save at poor second-hand through the medium of thought and its many forms. We do our best with symbols, and words are symbols of agreed, though imperfectly agreed, meaning. When, therefore, it is desired to transmit to another a spiritual experience, the first must descend to the level of thought and wrap his discovery in the opaque material of symbol in order to hand it to his friend. The friend must unwrap the symbol and absorb into his own understanding whatever is left of the direct experience, for him no longer direct. How, for example, can we enform, much less transmit, the 'flow' of a river? Not by removing a bucket of water, for there is no flow in that. By analogy, symbol and other forms and even gestures we may attempt the task, but we shall succeed but poorly. For the concept is but a symbol, and twice at least Carl Jung has pronounced the tremendous statement, that a concept is not a carrier of life. He says it first in discussing 'Society' which, as he points out, 'is nothing more than the concept of the symbiosis of a group of human beings. A concept is not a carrier of life. The sole and natural carrier of life is the individual and this holds true throughout nature.'[1] He returns to the same theme in his latest work, *The Undiscovered Self* (p. 75) where he is again extolling the value of the individual as against his thought creation of the State. 'The only direct and concrete carrier of life', he says, 'is the individual personality, while society and the State are conventional ideas. . . .'

Thought, then, has its limitations, and can no better convey ideas, the life force of thought, than a speech or essay can convey the beauty of a sunset. Nevertheless the thought machine can be, and should be in all, a most lovely instrument for its limited purposes. The analogy of the searchlight always comes to mind. It can be minutely directed, and nothing without its ambit is seen at all. It can be held indefinitely and when not wanted can be entirely switched off. How many can use that analogy for their own thinking minds?

Concrete and abstract thought

But thought functions on two distinguishable levels, concrete and abstract. The mind with which we arrange an appointment or buy the food for dinner is not that which we use in the higher ranges of a metaphysical discussion, or even in our appreciation of great art. And just as the 'lower' and 'higher' aspects of the mind are merged without any clear dividing line, so the faculty

[1] *Essays on Contemporary Events*, p. 31.

next beyond thought suffuses and illumines the higher ranges of our thinking. It is thus, I believe, that the next step beyond thought may be deliberately taken. As thought moves higher, in mathematics, philosophy, music and a hundred other fields of concept, the light of the intuition irradiates the thinker's mind, and the intuitive thinker is probably the highest product of *homo sapiens*. What, then, is this new faculty, the functioning of which can never be understood until the limitations of that next below it, the intellect or thought-machine, are thoroughly understood? It is not new to the West. In the East it is known as Buddhi and as such is the means of contacting Bodhi, Wisdom as distinct from knowledge. But the West is slow to appreciate it as utterly distinct in quality from the power of reasoning. Even the most advanced psychologists still find difficulty in accepting the intuition as more than a special department of thought, and it is the philosophers who are nearest to its true condition. In an interesting article on 'Intuition in Indian Philosophy' in the *Aryan Path*, Dr Gurumurti points out how Western philosophers, including Spinoza, Leibnitz, Hume, Kant, Hegel and Bergson, all admitted, explicitly or by implication, that reasoning alone could never reach Reality. For the intellect must work with the distinctions of the Knower, the Known and the Knowledge obtained, the inescapable trinity of any pair of the Opposites and the relation between them. It needs some faculty distinct in functioning to achieve direct cognition of Tathata, Suchness, the nature of things as they are, the Essence of Mind itself. The supreme purpose of all thought is indeed to prepare for the development of the intuition. Thought, in the sense of the highest thinking, literally clears the way of obstruction; then the light comes.

The Intuition

Intuition, then, is a faculty as distinct from thinking as thinking is from feeling and sensation, though all alike are functions of the individual mind which is in turn a reflection of All-Mind. In one sense it may be true, as Dr Radhakrishnan seems to suggest, that we can think so hard and rapidly that the steps of thought are taken, as it were, in a single leap, and we arrive at a creative understanding. This, indeed, is the process in sword-play, as expressed by the sword-masters of Japan. To think out what one's opponent is about to do, and how one will counter it, is death, for in the interval the blow will fall. The processes of thought and its translation into action must be so fused that thought becomes no-thought, and the first time that in fencing the blow so falls on one's opponent is a moment of Zen. But mere speed of thought is not intuition; it may be a way of approach, but in the end the flash (and all at all times use that word), is unmistakable, and incommunicable. If it is true, as Eckhart says, that we must achieve a 'transformed knowledge, and that it is by knowing that we get to this un-knowing', still, the unknowing is not in the world of thought, but beyond it.

The knowledge obtained by the intuition is direct, as direct as that obtained when salt is laid on the tongue. It is not, like emotion and thought, a reaction to or digestion of direct ex-perience. It knows on its own plane as directly as the eye knows a flash of lightning. And it knows all at once, not seriatim, even as the garden at night is totally lit by the lightning's flash. But intuitive knowledge is, as it were, four dimensional. In the same analogy we see the garden from all points of view at once. And, stranger still, none knows; there is no sense of a knower who knows what is seen. There is a fusion of knower and knowing with what is known, as distinct from the slow arrival of logic, by way of tested thesis, antithesis and logical progression to a point which may yet be discarded in the light of further thought.

Intuitive knowledge is at the moment of awareness pure, in the sense that it is unstained by evaluation or interpretation. These may come later, the labels of good and bad or right and wrong, of this meaning or that, being added by the thinking mind in its attempt to translate the experience into concept. Yet this moment is the degradation of the experience. The living life is shut into the boxes of concept, the flow of the river con-fined in a bucketful of its water, the glory of the sunset tran-scribed in paint on to a piece of canvas.

But the least flash of the intuition blurs the distinctions which are the stock in hand of thought, including that between the best and the worst of us. We are all compounded marvellously of good and evil, and it is a strange fact that we do not love one another for our strength so much as our weakness, for the small yet in some way lovable faults which we scarce know we display. I have long puzzled over this fact, and now am helped by Dr Jung's remarks in his battle cry for individual freedom, *The Undiscovered Self*. 'A human relationship', he says at pp. 104–5, 'is not based on differentiation and perfection, for these only emphasize the differences or call forth the exact opposite: it is based, rather, on imperfection, on what is weak, helpless and in need of support—the very ground and motive of dependence. The perfect has no need of the other, but weakness has. . . .'

For the intuition blurs all difference, and awakens reason itself to an awareness of the oneness behind the distinctions of phenomena. This 'coincidence of contraries' is at first an offence to thought, but thought must be willing to die into its own transcendence. As Aldous Huxley writes, 'In the last analysis the use and purpose of reason is to create the internal and external conditions favourable to its own transfiguration by and into spirit.'[1] In Eckhart's terms, 'we cannot conceive God for God is better than anything that we can conceive'. It is this that I have elsewhere called the Higher Third of the opposites. In terms of Yes and No it is the Zen Master's eager and im-mediate, 'Yes, yes' to any and every question. It is thus the supreme affirmation which neither affirms nor denies, the 'Nothing Between' as Mrs L. C. Beckett calls it in her *Neti Neti*. For intuitive knowledge lies between either-or, between all alternatives, and this Nothing-between is the goal of the Koan exercise. As the Zen Master Tai-hui used to say to his pupils, holding up his Hossu, a short stick, 'If you call this a stick you affirm; if you do not call it a stick, you negate. Beyond affirmation and negation what would you call it?' The answer, of course, is that you cannot call it anything. But you can know it, intuitively.

The qualities of intuitive awareness

A flash of intuitive awareness is unmistakable, and its qualities, universally agreed, are certainty, universality or a sense of

[1] *The Perennial Philosophy*, p. 163.

oneness, and the fact that the knowledge so gained is indescribable and incommunicable save in some irrational way. For communication must work by symbols, as already pointed out, the most common being sounds or printed words with an agreed meaning. But no symbol can completely express the truth for which it stands, and in the use of symbol there is always such loss in transmission as leaves in the hands of the receiver but a fragment of the truth which the transmitter had attained.

As a faculty usable at will the intuition is a rare attainment, though all possess·it in embryo. As Huang Po says, 'Those who seek the goal through cognition are like the fur (many) while those who obtain intuitive knowledge of the Way are like the horns (few).'[1] Yet there are those who believe that it is the next faculty to be developed by mankind. From the senses through the emotions to pure thinking; then beyond, to that which fuses thought into pure perception. So far it is paralysed in the West, for education ignores it, but it will surely come.

Dr Suzuki has called Enlightenment 'an act of intuition born of the will', and the effort needed to transcend the barriers of concept is great indeed. Yet the immediate effects of the effort are well worth while. What are the symptoms of awakening Buddhi? As I wrote in answer to this question in my own *Walk On!*, 'the faculty is dormant in all of us but, like unused muscles, needs developing. It belongs to the plane of union, synthesis, just as the intellect is the instrument of analysis and discrimination. It makes its awakening known, therefore, in a greater willingness to see the oneness of things, a shift of balance from differences to similarities, to life itself from the manifold forms which it uses and casts away. It shows in a certainty of decision, a feeling of "rightness" in all action while at the same time "sitting loose to life" in Geraldine Coster's immortal phrase. There is an inner sense of perpetual flow, a quiet acceptance of change and its consequent suffering, and a firm refusal to allow the mind to be stuck any longer in even its favourite beliefs and principles. There is a new direction towards essentials, and a corresponding indifference to trivialities. The usual preoccupation with problems, how to get round them or over them, gives way to a placid walking

[1] *The Zen Teaching of Huang Po*, translated by John Blofeld, p. 32.

through them, whereon, like the mist which lies on the roadway far ahead, they are often found to be non-existent.' The intuition brings tolerance, for as consciousness withdraws from its preoccupation with the daily round of phenomena, and retires deeper and deeper within itself, it is less concerned with means and devices and far more with the goal. It therefore extends to others a limitless tolerance, born of understanding of the way along which others seek the Truth. For 'the ways to the One are as many as the lives of men', and in the light of a new-born wisdom the awakening student sees this to be true. And in Dr Bendit's valuable phrase, 'Insight alone gives that illumination which makes knowledge live.'[1] Hence the distinction of knowledge *about* which may be taught in schools, and direct knowledge, which is wisdom, which is better learnt from heart to heart, from more enlightened to less enlightened men.

But just as emotion has its language, of poetry and music, and reason speaks in terms of concept and well ordered thought, so Buddhi has its own language of analogy, parable and simile, which say so much more than mere description. And of these new means for the conveyance of understanding, one is paradox which, as R. H. Blyth points out, 'does not spring from a desire to mystify the hearers or oneself. It arises from the inability of language to say two things at once. . . . The paradox is itself an example of what it teaches. The meaning escapes the words.'[2] Thus only, he says, the unsayable is said.

How, then, do we develop the faculty of intuition, existing in all of us, developed in so few? On the assumption that we have it, let us look for its manifestations. Surely we have all at times had a 'hunch' which fought against reason, and proved right, a sudden flash of understanding which made sense of conflicting thoughts and argument. The anonymous authors of *Some Unrecognized Factors in Medicine*, after talking of the use of intuition in medical diagnosis, go on to say, 'The same faculty is used by the scientist, philosopher or artist when, having given the best of his ordinary thinking to a problem, tension is released, and a leap made to a new and usually deeper and wider view of the whole matter. This ability to jump to a

[1] *The Psychic Sense*, p. 183.
[2] *Zen in English Literature*, pp. 180 and 183.

"new" field is perhaps in itself what we mean by intuition.[1] And the use of the word jump is a distinguishing factor in all intuitive experience. For no thinking in itself, however quick, will lead into intuitive knowledge. Always there is the effort, the giving way and the jump, and always the flash is sudden, unexpected, and beyond control. But when it comes it should be grasped and used. We should have, in the bold words of the Bhikshu Sangharakshita, 'the courage not of our intellectual convictions but of our transcendental realizations'.[1] At least let us provide this new profound knowledge with a chance to prove itself. Back it, if need be against reason, and see if reason does not in the end give way and agree. But this is no place to discuss ways of developing the intuition. Those who would seek such guidance as I can give will find it in the last few pages of my *Zen Buddhism*. It is enough to make clear that the intuition and this power alone can guide the seeker of right action to the final stage of Direct Action.

[1] p. 130.
[2] *A Survey of Buddhism*, p. 218.

Chapter 15

Direct Action

The Perfect Act has no Result

DIRECT action is the goal of all previous effort in the analysis of action. But the closer we approach direct action, which alone, by our analysis, is 'right', the more difficult is it to say anything useful about it. For words are but symbols of reality, so many fingers pointing to the moon, and direct action is largely that which has telescoped or utterly avoided the factors which would have made it indirect. Two men, walking down the street, in conversation, notice that another walking in front of them drops his umbrella. One of the two, without breaking the conversation, stoops and picks it up as he reaches it, and hands it to the third man who had paused to recover it. There are polite words of thanks and the two men, almost without breaking step, continue on their way. Here is direct action, and from the viewpoint of the men concerned, all but the perfect act. There was no deliberation, no plan; no formulated motive and no thought; the time and place and the means were 'right', and not only was there no consideration of result but probably no memory that such an event had taken place. Should not our largest as our lightest action be so ordered? Here was an immediate response to the situation, so sudden, im-mediate and complete as to eliminate the self of the doer, all choosing between right and wrong, and the least thought of reward. Above all there was no theorizing; the experience was utterly first-hand. When a learner-driver first lets in the clutch of his car and feels it moving under him he knows much more of driving a car than a hundred hours of theory could have taught him, and the woman who cooks her first omelette knows more than all the cookery books in the world. Book knowledge has its uses, but its uses come to an end. It is in daily life in action and not in cerebral conclusions that situations are solved and things get done. All can advise us in this action, but 'You yourself must make the effort. (Even) Buddhas do but point the Way.'[1] 'Buddhism', wrote Dr Suzuki, 'is personal experience and not impersonal philosophy',[2] and in this experience each man learns first-hand and by himself alone. The same applies to every way of life which is truly a way and more than a dry collection of dogma. For 'truth repeated is no longer truth; it becomes truth again only when it has been realized by the speaker as an immediate experience'.[3] Or as Jung says, 'What is essential to us can only grow out of ourselves. When the white man is true to his instincts, he reacts defensively against any advice that one might give him. What he has already swallowed, he is forced to reject again as if it were a foreign body, for his body refuses to assimilate anything sprung from foreign soil . . . A way is only *the* way when one finds it and follows it oneself.'[4]

Western rediscovery of Eastern truths

This explains what long had puzzled me. There are profound truths in the field of philosophy, psychology and what is now called science which were clearly stated in the Buddhist scriptures at least two thousand years ago, and these have been available in English for some forty years. Yet the West, eagerly seeking for truth in these and kindred fields, ignored them. I longed to put copies in the hands of these worthy men, to tell them, years before science 'discovered' it, that 'matter' is but motion; years before psychology announced it, that the unconscious is the womb of thought; that the logical necessity for the 'unimpeded interdiffusion' of all particulars (Jijimuge) of Kegon philosophy has not as yet been reached by the finest Western philosopher; now I know better. The Buddhist can but cap each new discovery with the right quotation to suggest that here are fingers pointing to the moon which at least describe

[1] *Dhammapada*, v. 276.
[2] *Essays in Zen Buddhism*, Third Series, p. 178.
[3] Aldous Huxley: *Adonis and the Alphabet*, p. 36.
[4] *The Integration of the Personality*, p. 31-2.

a moon to be seen and studied. But the man who makes a discovery by himself knows more than all the Scriptures of any faith; he knows, whereas those who quoted did for the most part know about. His knowledge is direct knowledge acquired by direct action; theirs but second-hand. Thus with a book; many a book have I read and underlined in it exciting passages, adding them to my own rough index at the end. Years later, maybe, I have found this truth for myself as something shining new, and was amazed, on a re-reading of the book, to find so much that I did not know I knew. We come back, then, to the paramount need for self-knowledge, knowledge acquired by the tested application of belief, that is, by direct action, in which the doer and the deed are so 'interfused' that no room is left for motive, right or wrong, or thought, or the least thought of consequence. What, then, can be said about right action that is, in some way, in itself direct, and not mere words and symbols standing in the way?

Direct action

It is the nearest we can achieve to the perfect act. Cleansed of the limitations of motive, thought and planned result it becomes, in Blyth's description of religion, 'the infinite way we do finite things'. It is the shortest line between the doer and the deed and as such is sudden, immediate and complete. It is always felt as utterly 'right' (if thought or feeling be added afterwards), whether it be an apple casually eaten as we pass the dish, or a letter answered and posted without delay, or the total situation which, in a crisis, is totally accepted and therefore completely solved (and dissolved). This sense of satisfaction is at least excusable.

> And to admire
> The satisfaction of all true desire
> 'Twas to be pleased with all that God hath done:
> 'Twas to enjoy even all beneath the sun:
> 'Twas with a steady and immediate sense
> To feel and measure all the excellence
> Of things.[1]

[1] Blyth is I think quoting from Traherne in *Zen in English Literature*, p. 148.

Don't argue about it, say the Masters of life in every school of it, don't think about it and don't pause. Get on with it. In *A Year of Grace* Victor Gollancz quotes a Hasidic story which has always pleased me: 'Once when Rabbi Bunam honoured a man in his House of Prayer by asking him to blow the ram's horn, and the fellow began to make lengthy preparations to concentrate on the meaning of the sounds, the Rabbi called out: "Fool, go ahead and blow."' Which reminds one of the master Ummon's saying to his pupils: 'If you walk just walk. If you sit, just sit. But whatever you do, don't wobble.' As Blyth sums up, speaking of the Japanese poet, Basho. 'When Basho looked at an onion he saw an onion; when he looked at the Milky Way he portrayed the Milky Way; when he felt a deep, unnameable emotion, he said so. . . . In poetry, as in life itself, directness is all important.'[1]

Direct action eliminates so far as possible all preparation unless the preparation is itself the direct action needed. And the motive should be one with the action and the will which drives it. 'Art thou looking for God, seeking God with a view to thy personal good, thy personal profit? Then in truth thou art not seeking God.' Would that Eckhart might return to thunder that at certain students that I know who claim to be seeking Zen, for, as the *Bhagavad Gita* points out again and again, the motive for action must be in the action itself and not in the event. And the means will come to hand and be the right means in the hand of the right man. 'Freedom is doing what you like, but freedom is Zen and Zen means liking what you do.'[2] Is not happiness doing what you want to do and wanting to do precisely what you do?

Direct seeing

At present we are sadly indirect in nearly all our actions, fogged with emotion, hesitant, tangled in a web of concept, doubtful of purpose, vague about result; selfish, though refinedly, from beginning to end. We cannot even see straight, physically or mentally. Sight is notoriously inaccurate, and all our seeing is conditioned by our thought. We have not learnt, as an artist learns, to look at things and flowers and faces, still less to see

[1] *Zen in English Literature*, p. 58.   [2] Ibid., p. 236.

them without added thought and value and desire. But we must see things as they are, and then as they were before distinction and difference were born, in that suchness or Tathata which is at once the unique nature of each thing and that which it shares in common with all other things that are. Only when we can see straight, that is, see things and situations as they are, can we act directly to them. Only such 'seeing is experiencing, seeing things in their state of suchness (Tathata) or is-ness. Buddha's whole philosophy comes from this "seeing".'[1]

There is a famous saying in Chinese Zen which is pertinent to this seeing. 'In the beginning mountains are seen as mountains and trees as trees. When we have gone a little way mountains are no longer seen as mountains nor trees as trees. But when we attain our enlightenment mountains are once more seen as mountains and trees as trees.' For the mountain we see at present does not, as science and philosophy agree, though for different reasons, exist. Even as the star whose light we 'see' may have ceased to exist some millions of years ago, so the mountain is a conglomeration of 'forms of motion' and has no being save in the world of becoming which is not Reality. Thus for a while we are in misery; nothing is real or true, but fleeting, changeable and inseparable from suffering. Then comes enlightenment, at least the first flash of it, and in its light all things are seen anew. The mountain is not, yet it is; for its Tathata, the 'suchness' or 'isness' of its essential mountainness is seen as such and as one with the Void in which all things are separately/One. And in this sudden light there is relief and laughter, and the mountain and the trees and all about them are right and lovely. As the Chinese poet Li-Po used to say of the favourite subject for his poems, 'We never grow tired of each other, the mountain and I.' Yet the world is far more than the sum of its parts, or direct action would be metaphysically, mystically and actually impossible. But as Alan Watts points out, 'individual bodies are only the terms, the end-points, of relationships—in short, the world is a system of inseparable relationships and not a mere juxtaposition of things'.[2]

To see thus clearly is to drop what stands between us and the

[1] Suzuki: *Mysticism, Christian and Buddhist*, p. 37.
[2] *Nature, Man and Woman*, p. 170.

view. How can we truly see a tree when thoughts about it intervene, or a dog when we fear it will bite us, or an idea when we wonder how in action it will affect ourselves? Only by shedding plans and purpose, fears and loves and hates can we see what stands before us, whether a human being, a demand for tax or something nice to eat. And the shedding of impediments may be so complete that direct action is none at all. In his very personal book, *The Goose is Out*, W. J. Gabb relates a personal story. 'I was out walking with my little boy, then about three years old, when he fell in a puddle. He lay there hollering and I walked on. Passers by were aghast at my apparent indifference. In a minute he was running at my heels, and his face reflected the cosmic accusation of the Cross, "I was hurted and you didn't help me." I said "Big boys get up by themselves. I left you to get up by yourself and look! you're a big boy now."'[1]

Purposelessness

The result of this shedding is a move from complexity to simplicity, which, in spiritual values, is a sign of maturity. But if it is not too difficult to simplify action it is hard indeed to cope with purpose and to raise it nearer to the 'purposelessness' of No-Mind. Yet all purpose implies a hunger for something we have not got, and hence a desire of the self which is probably unworthy. Action so prompted is at least apt to be wrong, for we and the act should be one and im-mediate, without wondering on right and wrong or why we are acting. In the ideal there is a sense of a greater purpose. Tennyson may be right when he says that 'through the ages one increasing purpose runs'. Sir Edwin Arnold called it 'a Power divine which moves to good', and Trine talked of 'attaching one's belt to the power-house of the universe'. Is this the 'Other Power' of Shin Buddhism; is it true that allowing for the limits of religious phraseology, my will is only effective when it is God's will, and no longer merely mine? Gabb speaks of this power in his famous chapter on 'The Address to the Situation', and all the religions of the world agree that the Light comes with a total surrender of all that we have and think we are—to something greater than ourselves. Only when we surrender to the event, contented,

[1] Pp. 52-3.

purposeless, can we find that emptiness out of which comes what Takuan called 'the most wondrous unfoldment of doing'. Asked, 'Who is the wise man?' Epictetus answered, 'He who is content', and for those who have practised it a little there is indeed 'vast strength in no desire'. In Western life we are so conditioned to competitive strife for money, honours, power and a public name that the man who is content with what he has is a puzzle to his rivals. But his strength is greater than theirs. With nothing to lose he is, in the terms of the *Tao Tê Ching*, soft and weak, but 'the soft and weak can overcome the hard and strong', and 'weakness is the appliance of Tao'. By this weakness the man of Tao, or Zen or God, can cope with any situation.

The intuition

The control tower for direct action is of course the intuition, of which much has already been said. But as we approach, however slowly, the higher ranges of understanding, the limitations of thought become more galling, and the light of the intuition, however fitful, our only guide. 'Only those who realize how far intuition soars above the tardy processes of ratiocinative thought can form the faintest thought of that Absolute Wisdom which transcends the ideas of Time and Space.'[1] As such we must in modern parlance 'give it air'. And air is its home; we rightly talk of inspiration as the source of spiritual knowledge and of the power which creates our finest deeds, of thought or art or circumstance. Henry James speaks of 'the perfect presence of mind, unconfused, unhurried by emotion, that any artistic performance requires and that all, whatever the instrument, require in the same degree: the application in other words, clear and calculated, crystal-firm as it were, of the idea conceived in the glow of experience, of suffering, of joy'.[2] Here is the trinity of inspiration, the experience, and the linked-up sorrow/joy. It is Shiva's dance for the creation of the world, the shout of laughter when we land from the existential jump which follows a flash of Jijimuge, when we feel and know 'the

[1] H. P. Blavatsky in the Proem to *The Secret Doctrine*.
[2] Quoted from 'The Tragic Muse' in *Have you Anything to Declare?* by Maurice Baring, p. 189.

unimpeded interdiffusion of all particular things'. This is beyond both oneness and the many and we shall know it rarely. Yet we must condition the mind to receive it, for it is the source and the essence of right action; all else bears Karma, and whether it seems to us good or bad it holds the untrue self together until the debt is paid.

> 'In the higher realms of true Suchness
> There is neither self nor other.
> When direct identification is sought
> We can only say, Not Two.'

Such is the intuition, a lady who at present favours us at will and whom we may not yet command. As Aldous Huxley puts it, 'We cannot make ourselves understand; the most we can do is to foster a state of mind in which understanding may come to us.'[1] Meanwhile let us use it and trust it and learn to obey. And the right place is the market-place, the office and the home.

The job in hand, the object of direct action, is always, as mentioned in Chapter One, Here and Now and This. We do what we are doing here, though the here of today may be different from that of yesterday. The same applies to now. There is only now by the clock for anything we do, and our awareness of that now can be expanded into Now, the perpetual moment, the 'one-thought-moment' of Zen Buddhism, for there is nothing else we know.

> In this Period the Poet's Work is Done, and all the Great
> Events of Time start forth and are conceived in such a Period,
> Within a Moment, a Pulsation of the Artery.[2]

Eckhart knew it well. 'The Now-moment in which God made the first man and the Now-moment in which the last man will disappear, and the Now-moment in which I am speaking are all one in God, in whom there is only one Now.'[3] Dr Benoit complains of a Western author on Zen who affirmed that a man liberated by Satori can do anything in any circumstances; but

---

[1] *Adonis and the Alphabet*, p. 65.
[2] From Blake, quoted in *The Fire and the Fountain*, John Press, p. 1.
[3] Trans. Blakney.

this, he says, 'is radically contrary to a true understanding, for the man liberated by Satori can only perform one single action in a given circumstance. He can no longer do anything but the action that is totally adequate to that circumstance; and it is in the immediate spontaneous elaboration of this unique adequate action that the enjoyment of the perfect liberty of this man lies.'[1] In one sense that is an abuse of the word circumstance, but in another it is true that in the appropriate and solely adequate right action in a given situation there is an element of determinism, made up of the inevitable right result of a thousand actions bearing Karma by the actor faced with such a circumstance.

The job in hand

For direct action is solely concerned with the job in hand, whatever that may be. Whether we call it work or play, or whether it is strenuous or a period of repose, it is the next job to be done and should therefore be done immediately, that is, without any mediating factor of emotion or thought. How it is done is a question of method, which is of secondary importance. 'Zen's first concern is about its experience and not its modes of expression', says Dr Suzuki, and Zen technique is the most direct action that we know.[2] 'When occupations come to us we must accept them; when things come to us, we must understand them from the ground up.'[3] In a recent interview, reported in the *Sunday Times*, Mr Aldous Huxley said that Zen Buddhism appealed to him as a religion which reconciles humanism and mysticism, a transfiguration of the world which is not an escape from it. And in a letter to the author he speaks of 'the practice of being conscious of immediate and unconceptualized experience'. This is the secret, to acquire such experience, and not to spoil this garden of delight with the ugly tin shed of concept, either before or after. Must we mar a glorious symphony, a nice cup of tea or the making of a new friend with chatter, silent or expressed, about it and about? Can we not learn to flow with the experience? 'While moving and changing

---

[1] *The Supreme Doctrine*, p. 65.
[2] *Mysticism, Christian and Buddhist*, p. 59.
[3] *The Secret of the Golden Flower*, p. 57.

one must become the moving and changing';[1] while in it we *are* the experience, yet never bound by it. 'Do not permit the events of your daily lives to bind you, but never withdraw yourselves from them';[2] this is the ideal, to be 'in the world yet not of it', thus is the act performed and the actor free.

Paradoxically enough, the actor becomes free in proportion to his becoming impersonal and at the same time acting with the whole of himself in all he does. John Press, in his analysis of inspiration in poetry says that a great poem must express with complete fidelity the personal vision of the poet. 'The more piercing, exact, coherent and complex the vision, the greater the poem, but the essence of the vision is its individuality, its undistorted reflection of the total experience of one man. The presentation of a set of dogmas, held even with complete sincerity, can never be a substitute for this personal experience in which belief and doubt, passion and thought, memory and desire are so closely blended that nobody can distinguish the one from the other.'[3] Teachers please note—but psychologists would heartily agree. No act is well done when done with half the man, nor directly done when a part of him hangs back, or is suppressed by the rest, or has never been developed. At the moment the actor is a complex selfhood, part self, the 'shadow' of the true man, part Self, the Jekyll to this Hyde, the 'better' part of him, and part, or partly a conscious reflection of the SELF, which is no one man and no man's property. The process must continue, therefore, one way or the other—it matters not which for the result is the same—for the self to be nothing or the SELF to be all. Ramakrishna tells a story of Sankaracharya and one of his disciples who complained that he got nò instructions. 'Once when Sankara was seated alone, he heard the footsteps of someone coming behind. He called out, "Who is there?" The disciple answered, "It is I."' The Acharya said, 'If the word "I" is so dear to thee, then either expand it indefinitely, that is, know the universe as thyself, or renounce it altogether',[4] or as Edwin Arnold puts it 'Forgoing self, the universe grows I.'

[1] Suzuki: *Mysticism, Christian and Buddhist*, p. 99.
[2] *The Zen Teaching of Huang Po*, p. 131.
[3] *The Fire and the Fountain*, p. 35.
[4] *The Bible of the World*, edited by Robert Ballou, p. 170.

As all is changing, the parts of the self included, some part of self is dying daily, hourly, momentarily. And always illusion dies to Reality. 'Every actual experience is a little death, the extinction of self-consciousness. And it is this little death, which is the entering into the wholeness of the experience of the "moment", that Zen emphasizes . . .'[1] and Dr Suzuki quotes Jacques Maritain as saying, 'The creative self is both revealing itself and sacrificing itself, because it is *given*; it is drawn out of itself in that sort of ecstasy which is creation, it dies to itself in order to live in the work (how humbly and defencelessly).'[2] For life and death are but another of the pairs of opposites. Hence Shakespeare's deep advice:

> 'Be absolute for death: either death or life
> Shall thereby be the sweeter.'

The Japanese Samurai warrior 'died' before he went into battle, so that this illusion at least should not affect his arm in the service of his Lord.

Yet all direct action is not fierce, or even positive. It is true that all attainment needs effort, if only to 'let go'. But, as already shown, these are another of the Pairs, and as Dr Suzuki wrote, 'life moves in its complete oneness whether restlessly or serenely as you may conceive it; your interpretation does not alter the fact. Zen takes hold of life in its wholeness and moves "restlessly" with it or stays quietly with it.' But 'the tranquility of Zen is in the midst of boiling oil, the surging waves, and in the flames enveloping the god Acala'.[3]

The effects of direct action

But whether the act be direct in its positive or negative sense, in doing the right thing or in rightly doing nothing, the cumulative effect on the man of direct action and his effect on others is soon apparent. There is an increased directness of communication with all sensitive minds, and the man concerned becomes 'great' by what he humbly is rather than by the trappings of success accorded him by those about him. This is

[1] Gai Eaton: *The Richest Vein*, p. 114.
[2] *Creative Intuition in Art and Poetry*, p. 107.
[3] *Zen Buddhism and its Influence on Japanese Culture*, p. 229

presumably the meaning of Emerson's famous phrase; 'What you are speaks so loudly that I cannot hear what you say', and though such a man may be 'as nothing in the eyes of men', he becomes, as it were, a catalytic agent which, itself doing nothing, precipitates others into actions true to themselves. The balance of such men on the subtle and knife-edge Middle Way enables them to be at once teachers and pupils, learning hard while teaching all they know. Having to a large extent dissolved their shields of self-importance, their masks of an untrue face to circumstance, they are what they are contentedly, and the light as they have found it shines the more sweetly for their fellow men.

As such they are living witness to their own experience; they point, and smile, but seldom explain, for as Dr Spiegelberg points out, 'the trouble with explanations is that, being limited to the phenomena they take into account, they cannot deal with evidence beyond their scope. They are of value only within the frame of reference of their own terminology or point of view'.[1] And a point of view is always a limitation. 'Great' Christians or Buddhists or Jews are great beyond the limitations of their several viewpoints. They are men who know, and what they *know* is quite remarkably the same. They cannot explain this knowledge, at once the cause and fruit of direct action. Asking why he should bathe in the river as directed, a monk was told, 'Just a dip and no why.' And just as direct action can alone find truth, however called, so only direct action can express its discovery. That is why Zen Masters, for example, act in the strange way they do. It is not that they want to be mysterious or enigmatic or absurd, but the pupil's bonds of thought can never be broken in their own terms; argument and explanation can never break the fetters of argument and thought. The Masters did and do what they do because there is no other way of doing what they want to do, to bring the pupil into direct relations with Reality; and Reality to them is as visible in a lump of earth as in an image of the Buddha, and in drinking tea with a friend far more than in psychic states induced by hours of meditation. 'The Master Yen-jui came up to the pulpit, the monks crowded into the hall, the master rose

[1] *Living Religions of the World*, p. 10.

from his seat and danced and said, "Do you understand?" "No, Master", the monks answered. Yen-jui demanded, "I performed, without abandoning my religion, a deed belonging to the world; why do you not understand?" [1] Could words say more?

If this be too 'Japanese', here is a Western student's story to the same effect. 'Yengu had made the arduous journey over the mountains to a sheltered valley where grew the rarest lilies. He was now returned to the monastery which was perched upon high bleak rocks. "How could you leave such a warm place to return to this?" asked Lung, shivering in the cold wind. "I wanted to gather lilies," replied Yengu. Or again, "I seek enlightenment", said the fair pupil after serving tea to the senior student. "Then wash up" he replied. "I have." There was silence. "I see" said the pupil. "You see nothing—yet." "I see." "That's better", said the older student, "but why not wash up?" '

[1] Quoted by Dr Suzuki in *Essays in Zen Buddism*. Third series, pp. 41–20

Chapter 16

Non-Action

Be humble and you will remain entire
TAO TÊ CHING

I F it was difficult to say anything useful of direct action it is all but impossible to speak of Non-Action. 'The Tao that can be expressed is not the eternal Tao.' For here is the threshold of No-Mind, of Prajna-consciousness, of the Void. The difficulty is that of seeing one's eyes, or of lifting oneself up by one's belt. For we must reach No-Mind by the path of mind, slay the tyranny of concept by means of the concept-machine. Put conversely, the problem is worse still. 'You must use', said Huang Po, 'the wisdom which comes from non-dualism to destroy your concept-forming, dualistic mentality'[1]—Or, as *The Voice of the Silence* has it, 'The mind is the great slayer of the Real: let the disciple slay the slayer.'

Acting 'as if'
The task is formidable, but it has to be done. To help, I humbly offer a practice I have found most helpful. It has, like other ways to Truth, its dangers of abuse and misunderstanding; it also has its rewards. I call it acting 'as if'. The imagination, the image-building faculty of the mind, is the principal tool of man's creation; all that he makes, whether breakfast, a railway line or an Act of Parliament, is preceded by the imagination, the visualization of the thing made. True, the perfect act cuts out this planning stage, but we are seeking ways to the perfect act. Just as we may think of ourselves sunning our bodies on a summer holiday, and then make plans for doing it, so we can imagine ourselves in a chosen state of

[1] *The Zen Teaching of Huang Po*, p. 115.

mind, as a useful step to attaining it. Having imagined ourselves, for example, as utterly serene in a situation which would normally upset us, whether domestic, at the dentist, or taking the chair at an annual meeting, we proceed to behave 'as if'. This is not the same as the advice of Dr Coué. Here there is no attempt to bludgeon the sub-conscious into accepting as true what the conscious knows to be false; it is quietly stepping into the state of mind which, if the teaching of the masters of the Wisdom be true, we essentially are. 'For you must know,' said Hui-neng, if I may quote him again, 'that so far as Buddha-nature is concerned, there is no difference between an enlightened man and an ignorant one. What makes the difference is that one realizes it while the other does not.'[1] We *are* serene, all-knowing, 'awakened', 'enlightened', compassionate, free, as the masters of life point out. If, therefore, we have not yet rediscovered the fact by direct experience, let us act as though we had, and thus be genuinely more serene, more certain-minded, more direct in action than before. There are many ways of climbing a mountain. The Zen way is to begin at the top which, though irrational, is strangely practical. When the reigning Abbot of Myoshinji, the mother temple of Rinzai Zen Buddhism in Japan, wished for a mighty dragon to be painted on the ceiling of the principal building he sent for the artist and gave his command. 'But I have never seen a dragon', said the artist unhappily, and he went away to find someone who had. He failed to find anyone, and returned to say so. 'Become the dragon', said the Abbot. And there it is, a mighty flaming monster for all to see. If we cannot yet attain this simple direct-ness of action we can at least try. We all know the old joke— 'Can you play the violin?' 'I don't know, I've never tried'— but shall we ever play the fiddle until we do—try? And to be serene, why not just be—serene? Perched on that pinnacle, though expecting any moment to fall off, things do indeed look different. The violent pendulum of like/dislike slows down; there is a sense of timelessness, in the sense of freedom from the tyranny of time; of flowing happily with the rhythm of life, of accepting all things as quite obviously 'right'. The same applies to strength, if that is needed, or the power to

[1] *The Sutra of Wei lang*, p. 27.

heal. We have it all so why not act 'as if'? Why not waken here and now to what we are, and live accordingly, remembering that 'a man believes a thing when he behaves as if it were true'? This may be psychologically unsound, but I find that it works, in myself and others, and even if I need the attentions of a trained psychiatrist I shall resist all treatment, content for the while to retain such a useful disease.

New use of concept

In the approach to Non-action concept more and more becomes an instrument to be used as needed and then laid down. It is of supreme use on its own plane and useful to rationalize, make reasonable, the increasing functioning of the intuition. Meanwhile the limitations of thought are increasingly seen. The mind attempts with increasing success to conceive action and inaction as a pair of opposites; then to conceive a state which is at the same time energetic and accepting, passive/strenuous. But a state which is neither active nor passive, neither neither nor both . . . ? The brain staggers and halts in its pursuing; the mind cannot conceive. Now Prajna, the Zen intuition of self-identity, takes over (or maybe for a while Prajna-as-if), and the Void has at least the semblance of life-giving meaning. This is the product of renewed attempts at dropping all manner of clinging, to the wants of self but also to the wants of Self, to evil and to good, to Samsara and also to Nirvana. To this understanding all devices and means are equally useful, and useless. As Alan Watts puts it, 'There is no way to where we are, and whoever seeks one finds only a wall of granite without passage or foothold. Yogas, prayers, therapies and spiritual exercises are at root only elaborate postponements of the recognition that there is nothing to be grasped and no way to grasp it.'[1] This is a hard truth, but until we learn to flow, to stop clinging to either bank of the river, to let go heaven as well as hell, we shall not be walking on to the goal which is here already.

The attention is once more focused on the self which clings, which creates and bears the illusions. It is remarkable how many problems and situations cease to produce the emotions of fear,

[1] *Nature, Man and Woman*, p. 108.

anxiety and doubt as soon as the factor of self is deliberately abstracted. So long as I consider 'I' in any problem, there will be action, probably wrong. No-action begins where the 'I' factor ceases to operate. For the suffering self there can be no therapy. Worries, quarrels, futile argument—the whole gamut of love and hate, all these and their attendant medicines will fade away when the cause of them is removed, and not before. One cannot heal the knife that stabs one; we cannot heal a problem as such. But we can and should remove the factor which made it a problem, the wants and the fears and the loves of 'I'. As we more and more drop self, the sense of a separate ego with its 'feelings', pride and restless will to expand like a balloon, we shall stand the more naked to the winds of circumstance but, strangely enough, the winds will blow straight through us, and the results be nil. To leave the house of self for a while is like leaving a stuffy, noisy and unprofitable party. How sweet the cool night air and the space about one! And for some the technique of dropping self is to merge, with joy, into the larger life of others. 'Nirvana is where the Bodhisattva stages are passed through one after another, is where compassion for others transcends all thoughts of self. . . . It is where the manifestation of noble wisdom that is Buddhahood expresses itself in perfect love for all. . . .'[1]

The method of 'As if' may be applied to things as yet too high for us to grasp entirely as they are, but in imagination at least we must learn to see them as they were before the illusion of duality was born, before the bifurcation into the opposites took place. 'A monk asked, "What is the one word?" "What do you say?" said the master. "What is the one word?" the monk repeated. Said the master, "You make it two."'

The logic of the intuition

Then comes the paradox for the Western mind. There is only one, not two; but the one is two and all things. A is A, says the logician. A is also not-A says the man of Zen, with maddening Zen logic. A is A is reasonable; A is also not-A is quite unreasonable, but in its wild unreason it sets us free from the domination of thought. 'The ordinary logical process of reason-

[1] From the *Lankavatara Sutra*.

ing is powerless to give final satisfaction to our deepest spiritual needs. Zen declares that words are words and no more. When words cease to correspond with facts it is time for us to part with words and return to facts.'[1] And in facts we shall find 'As if' come true. If the concepts of light and darkness fail to illumine, use a candle. One evening Te-shan was sitting outside the master's room, earnestly in search of truth. 'Why do you not come in?' asked Ch'ung-hsin, the master of the monastery. 'It is dark', replied Te-shan. Whereupon Ch'ung-hsin lighted a candle and handed it to him. When Shan was about to take it Hsin blew it out. This suddenly opened Shan's mind to the truth of Zen. He bowed respectfully. . . .

The birth of spontaneity

With the approach to Non-Action, there is a new sense of spontaneity in action, as of a natural, almost casual flow with the stream of events in a ceaseless becoming which, though flowing in a world of illusion, is none the less entirely real. Gone is the sense of suppression, of acting or non-acting from external stimulus alone. Now at last you can be natural. Yell with rage if you wish to, and at the dentist if you must be hurt, be hurt. Hate or love when you hate or love; wonder always, and when you want to, doubt. There will be no more false solemnity, at death or sudden change. Cry in grief if you will, but laugh to follow; and play the fool as occasion moves you. Goethe was right:

> 'We mortals are most wonderfully tried,
> Nor could we bear it were we not vouchsafed
> By Nature a divine frivolity.'[2]

For if all that exists is, as Buddhist philosophy demands, unreal and changing rapidly, why take it seriously? No man can do more harm to you than to advance the date of your body's death, nor affect in the least a mind that has become, by shedding self, proof against adversity. What, then, is important? Only the job in hand, whatever it may be. To sew on a button that needs sewing now is far more important than playing with the

[1] Suzuki: *An Introduction to Zen Buddhism*, p. 47.
[2] Translated in Maurice Baring's *Have you Anything to Declare?* p. 180.

concept of tomorrow's business or the memory of last night's party. It is a great relief to find that we can accept all things for what they are, and even as they seem to be, whether miracles, tragedies, absurdities or grief. Even idleness, for is not one of the greatest of Zen paintings that of an old man playing cat's cradles with a piece of string looped over his toe? The caption speaks for itself—'Busy being idle'. What, it may be asked, is, in the last analysis, more important?

All things now are seen as 'nothing special'. In the words of the old Chinese poem,

> Mount Lu in misty rain; the river Che at high tide;
> When I had not been there, no rest from the pain of longing.
> I went there and returned . . . it was nothing special—
> Mount Lu in misty rain; the river Che at high tide.[1]

This is why those who have attained discount even their own Satori. It is 'nothing special'. All is taken as it is, used, dropped and forgotten. When all is felt as undivided how shall there be unfriendliness, or a fierce exclusive friendliness? We may even now be care-less. Does care, in the sense of emotion about the unchangeable, assist any living thing? Shall we not join Coventry Patmore in 'the little bay' wherein he sat to watch as 'the purposeless, glad ocean comes and goes'?

> For want of me the world's course will not fail:
> When all its work is done, the lie shall rot;
> The truth is great, and shall prevail,
> When none cares whether it prevail or not.

With this the words of an English ballad come to mind:

> Only we'll sit awhile, as children play,
> Without tomorrow, without yesterday.

For children do not care for the falling leaf; should we for the falling tree? Or for the end of a career, or the passing of an age? Carelessly is a lovely word for the sage as he walks on

[1] By Sotoba of the Sung Dynasty. I have used the version in Alan Watts' *The Way of Zen* as more concise than that in Suzuki's *Essays in Zen Buddhism*, First Series, p. 12.

through the infinitely finite field of life. To some of us the unforgettable symbol of such living was Dr Suzuki and the young Mihoko Okamura, his pupil, secretary and friend, with sixty-five years between them, as they walked through Europe hand in hand, serene, content, at one with reality.

This is the ideal we approach, and an ideal is none the worse for being still a long way off. I like to think of the process as reducing the thickness of the walls about us that keep out the sun, remembering that we put them there. As the walls of the room in which we think grow thinner with our use of wider, nobler, more one-making thought, so they become transparent to the light, the light which we thought without us and now find within. We rightly speak of a great mind as illumined, brilliant, and of the Buddha as the All-Enlightened One. Slowly the walls grow thinner and the light more visible. With the light we see more, and more deeply understand. The Opposites approach one another more easily, producing a direct, spontaneous, natural way of living in which each situation is faced with the whole man utterly, contentedly, just 'walking on'.

Flashes true and false

Then come the flashes. As a student said, we scrape at the walls but know not at what moment we shall poke a finger through! But there are plenty of flashes that are not Satori. There are psychic visions without value and flashes of understanding where there was none before. But he who asks if such are Satori is answered; none who has that moment of awakening doubts; the experience provides its own authority. For the rest, we may argue of Dhyana, Samadhi and Prajna, but we argue in terms of concept; we do not as yet know. For the experience is a total transformation. Subtly, indescribably, the man is not as he was before. All things are seen as new; they are as they were, but the seeing is different. And the difference lies in the fusion of the man who sought and the awakening. None sought; none has attained—anything. In this absolute moment the subject/object are so one that he who has it knows it not; there is none to know. Afterwards, back in time, that is another matter. But then he can only smile; he cannot explain. He that knew 'life as it lives itself' continues, that much nearer than before, to live it. Only thus can he teach what now he knows. The rest is silence, and a finger pointing to the moon. Later will come another 'experience', then more. Not often, save for the few. But more of us may know 'the little enlightenments', as the great Hakuin called them. He describes the method of Introspection by which 'not only were my illnesses healed, but also all those things which are difficult to believe, difficult to penetrate, difficult to understand . . . those things I now understood intuitively at once, penetrating them to their roots, piercing them to their depths. Thus I experienced the great joy six or seven times. And besides this I forget how many times I have experienced the little enlightenments, the joys which make one dance . . .'[1]

The goal of Non-action

And the Goal? Who knows, nor does it greatly matter to us now. We can never know more of the Absolute than its manifestations; it is surely enough to attain that stage described in the *Bhagavad Gita* when all actions are 'consumed in the fire of knowledge'. For such knowledge, or Prajna, will be one with divine compassion, Karuna, when in the absence of all sentient beings to be delivered there will be no will to deliver. Even compassion bears the taint of duality, of one to help and one who needs our helping. In the ultimate Non-action there is none to save or to be saved. Meanwhile our present duty is clear, so to act that none shall suffer without our striving to remove its cause, whether the cause be without us or within.

> 'Let not the fierce sun dry one tear of pain before
> thyself has wiped it from the sufferer's eye.
> But let each burning human tear drop on thy heart
> and there remain; nor ever brush it off until the
> pain that caused it is removed.'[2]

From action right and wrong, but ever imperfect if not direct, and from direct action to that which lies beyond all action and inaction, Non-action, such is the progress from our human

---

[1] From Hakuin's *Yasen Kanna*, translated by the Rev. R. D. Shaw and Wilhelm Schiffer, S.J. in *Monumenta Nipponica*, Tokyo, Vol. XIII, p. 126.
[2] *The Voice of the Silence*.

point of view, and with the arrival of Non-action there is a return to Being, to that pole of 'isness' with which this book began. There are always those who say 'Why act—why not be content to be?' And the answer, as given in the Introduction, is that between our present muddled doing and the ideal of right Being there is a long, hard road to tread. The author of *Fingers Pointing Towards the Moon*, who writes as 'Wei-Wu-Wei', is right to begin at the top. 'Non-Action on the plane of Being becomes, by articulation, Correct-Action on the plane of the Existing.'[1] Granted, but the reverse path by which the Existing becomes again its 'suchness' of pure Being is one that all must tread. Huang Po describes the ideal. 'From thought-instant to thought-instant, no FORM; from thought-instant to thought-instant, no ACTIVITY—that is to be a Buddha! If you students of the Way wish to become Buddhas, you need study no doctrines whatever, but learn only how to avoid seeking for and attaching yourselves to anything. Where nothing is sought this implies Mind unborn; where no attachment exists, this implies Mind not destroyed; and that which is neither born nor destroyed is the Buddha.'[2] But how to attain to this Mind-unborn? I cannot accept the facile teaching of those who claim that all effort is needless and, indeed, defeats its own object. What is the alternative? Those whom I regard as the most spiritually advanced men I have ever met all bore the marks of a tremendous struggle; those who speak of 'no effort' are still to my understanding toying with concepts, often from the comfort of a hypothetical arm-chair. I agree with the anonymous author of *Splendour in the Night*. 'Always within, some sword point of my consciousness pierced through the fog and found first principles. Always within, something stirred and saved me from the level of content. I was to climb, we were all to climb, and doing the job at hand seemed to be the mountain offered for the scaling. Ascending hillsides; that was our function. Our means and our end.'[3] These are brave words, as from a master of right action. Asked, 'What is Tao?' a master of Zen replied, 'Walk on'!

[1] *Fingers Pointing Towards the Moon*, p. 3.
[2] *The Zen Teaching of Huang Po*, p. 40.
[3] *Splendour in the Night*. Published by John M. Watkins, 1933, p. 38.

BRIEF GLOSSARY

Sk = Sanskrit, P = Pali, Chin = Chinese, Jap = Japanese

ABHIDHAMMA (P). The third division of the Scriptures of the Theravada School of Buddhism. It contains an entire system of mind-training.

AHAMKARA. The conception of 'I', or the 'I'-illusion.

ANATTĀ (P), ANĀTMAN (Sk). The essentially Buddhist doctrine of non-ego.

ARHAT (P), ARHANT (Sk). One who has traversed the Eightfold path to the goal of Nirvana.

ĀTMAN (Sk), ATTĀ (P). The Supreme Self; Universal Consciousness.

AVIDYĀ (Sk), AVIJJĀ (P). Ignorance; lack of enlightenment.

BHAKTI (Sk). Devotion to a spiritual ideal. *Bhakti Yoga* is one of the three main divisions of *Rāja Yoga*, the other two being *Jnāna* (Wisdom) and *Karma* (Action).

BHĀVANĀ (Sk & P). Self-development by any means, but especially by the method of mind-control, concentration and meditation.

BHIKKHU (P), BHIKSHU (Sk). A member of the Buddhist *Sangha* (monastic Order).

BODHI (Sk). Enlightenment; the spiritual condition of a Buddha or Bodhisattva.

BODHISATTVA (Sk). One whose 'being' or 'essence' (*sattva*) is *Bodhi*. The Wisdom resulting from direct perception of Truth, with the compassion awakened thereby.

BRAHMA. One aspect of the threefold God-head of the Hindu pantheon.

BRAHMAN. The impersonal and supreme Principle of the Universe.

BUDDHA. A title meaning Awakened, in the sense of Enlightened. The founder of Buddhism in the sixth century B.C.

BUDDHI (Sk). The vehicle of Enlightenment (Bodhi). The faculty of direct awareness of Reality. The intuition.

DĀNA (Sk & P). Benevolence, giving, charity.

DEVA (Sk). A celestial being, good, bad or indifferent in nature; they correspond to the angelic powers of Western theology.

DHARMA (Sk), DHAMMA (P). System, doctrine, law, truth, cosmic order (according to the context). The Buddhist Teaching.

189

DHYĀNA (Sk). Supreme meditation. Direct absorption in Truth. The Japanese derivation of the word is ZEN which, however, has a very different meaning.

HOSSU (Jap). The stick or staff carried by a Zen Master.

JIJIMUGE (Jap). The doctrine of the Japanese Kegon School of the 'unimpeded interdiffusion' of all particulars.

JIRIKI (Jap). Salvation by one's own efforts. (c.f. Tariki).

JNĀNA YOGA. Wisdom Yoga. (c.f. Bhakti).

JUDO (Jap). First known as Ju-jitsu, this Japanese form of wrestling applies the principles of Taoism and Zen to physical contest.

KARMA (Sk), KAMMA (P). The Law of cause and effect, as applied to the mind. Karma is not limited by time and space, and is not strictly individual; there is group Karma, family, national, etc. The doctrine of Rebirth is an essential corollary to that of Karma.

KARUNĀ (Sk). Action compassive, c.f. *prajnā*

KENDO (Jap). The Japanese School of fencing.

KLESA (Sk). Defilement, defiling passions, the elimination of which is essential to progress on the Path.

MAHĀYĀNA. The Buddhist School of the Great Vehicle (of liberation); also called the Northern School (Tibet, Mongolia, China, Korea and Japan).

MANAS (Sk). Mind. The rational faculty in man.

MANTRA (Sk). A magical formula or invocation.

MUDRĀ (Sk). Ritual gestures of the hands used in symbolic magic. Buddha images are found in a variety of *mudrā* positions.

NIDĀNAS (P). The twelve *nidānas* are links in the chain of karmic causation, the Buddhist method of demonstrating the reign of law in the psycho-physical realms of existence.

NIRVĀNA (Sk), NIBBĀNA (P). The supreme goal of Buddhist endeavour; release from the limitations of separate existence. A state attainable in this life. One who has attained to this state is called *arhat*.

PALI. One of the early languages of Buddhism. It was later adopted by the Theravadins as the language in which to preserve the memorized teachings of the Buddha.

PĀRAMITĀS (Sk). Perfections. The six (or ten) stages of spiritual perfection followed by the Bodhisattva in his progress to Buddhahood.

PRAJNĀ (Sk), PANNĀ (P). Transcendental Wisdom. One of the *pāramitās*. One of the two pillars of the Mahāyāna, the other being *karuna* (compassion).

RUPA. Form, body. Also image, usually as an image of the Buddha.

SAMĀDHI. Contemplation on Reality. The eighth step on the Eight-fold Path.

SAMKHĀRAS (P), SAMSKĀRAS (Sk). Mental predispositions; the karmic results of mental illusion. One of the five *skandhas*, the second link in the Nidāna Chain.

SAMSĀRA (Sk & P). Continued 'coming-to-be'. Existence in the world as compared with Nirvana.

SANGHA. The Monastic Order founded by the Buddha. The third of the three jewels of *Buddha* (the Teacher), *Dhamma* (his Teaching) and *Sangha* (the Order).

SANNA (P). Perception; awareness of and assimilation of sensation. One of the five *skandhas*.

SATORI (Jap). The 'goal' of Zen Buddhism. A state of consciousness beyond the plane of discrimination and differentiation.

SĪLA (Sk & P). The Buddhist code of morality.

SKANDHA (Sk), KHANDA (P). The five causally-conditioned elements of existence forming a being or entity. They are inherent in every form of life, either in an active or a potential state.

SUNYATĀ (Sk). Voidness. The doctrine which asserts the Voidness of Ultimate Reality. It abolishes all concepts of dualism and proclaims the essential oneness of the phenomenal and the noumenal.

TAO (Chin). The central concept of Taoism, as expressed in the *Tao Tê Ching*. Can mean the One and the Way to it.

TARIKI (Jap). Salvation by 'Other Power', usually the personification of the Absolute. (c.f. *Jiriki*).

TATHĀGATA (Sk). A title the Buddha used of himself. He who has 'thus come and gone' (before), thus teaching the same Truth as his predecessors in title.

TATHATĀ (Sk). Lit. 'Thusness' or 'Suchness' (of things).

THERAVADA (P). The 'Doctrine of the Elders' who formed the first Buddhist Council. The School of Buddhism of Ceylon, Burma and Thailand.

TRISHNĀ (Sk), TANHĀ (P). Thirst for sentient existence; separative desire.

UPĀYA-KAUSĀLYA (Sk). Skill in the choice of means.

VEDANĀ (P). Sense reaction to contact. The seventh link in the twelve nidānas, the chain of causation, producing the craving or thirst for existence.

VIJNĀNA (Sk), VINNĀNA (P). Consciousness; the faculty by which one cognizes the phenomenal world.

WABI (Jap). A term used in Japanese art to describe a mood of 'spiritual loneliness'; a subjective state of poverty enjoyed.

WEI-WU-WEI (Chin). Action-non-action. More usually written as Wu-Wei. Meaning action in inaction.

WU-WEI (Chin). Action in inaction.

YĀNA (Sk & P). Vehicle or means of progress. As in Mahāyāna, the 'Great Vehicle' or Northern School of Buddhism.

YANG (Chin). The light, hard, creative, and male.

YIN (Chin). The dark, soft, receptive, and female.

YOGA. The Hindu system of discipline which brings a man to union (with Reality).

ZEN (Jap). A corruption of the Chinese *Ch'an* which in turn is derived from the Sanscrit *Dhyāna*. The School of Zen Buddhism which passed from China to Japan in the thirteenth to fourteenth centuries.

For further details see *A Buddhist Students' Manual* published by the Buddhist Society, 58 Eccleston Square, S.W.1.

BIBLIOGRAPHY

of works quoted

ABEGG, LILY: *The Mind of East Asia*. Thames & Hudson, 1952.

ANONYMOUS: *Some Unrecognized Factors in Medicine*. The Theosophical Publishing House, 1939. *Splendour in the Night*. Watkins, 1933.

ARBER, AGNES: *The Manifold and the One*. Murray, 1947.

ARNOLD, SIR EDWIN: *The Light of Asia*.

BALLOU, ROBERT: *The Bible of the World*. Viking Press, New York, 1939.

BAYNES, H. G.: *Analytical Psychology and the English Mind*. Methuen, 1950.

BECKETT, L. C.: *Neti Neti*. The Ark Press, 1955.

BENDIT, L. J., and PAYNE, P. D.: *The Psychic Sense*. Faber, 1943. *This World and That*. Faber, 1940.

BENOIT, H.: *The Supreme Doctrine*. Routledge & Kegan Paul, 1951.

The Bhagavad Gita: Trans. W. Q. Judge, United Lodge of Theosophists, 1920.

BLAVATSKY, H. P.: *The Voice of the Silence* (Trans.). Theosophical Publishing Co., 1889. *The Secret Doctrine*. Theosophical Publishing Co., 1888. *The Key to Theosophy*. Theosophical Publishing Co., 1889.

BLOFELD, J. (Trans.): *The Huang Po Doctrine of Universal Mind*. Rider, 1958.

BLYTH, R. H.: *Zen in English Literature and Oriental Classics*. The Hokuseido Press, 1942.

BOWEN, P. G.: *The Sayings of the Ancient One*. Rider, 1935.

CONZE, E.: *Buddhism*. Bruno Cassirer, 1951. *Selected Sayings from the Perfection of Wisdom*. The Buddhist Society, 1955.

COOMARASWAMY, ANANDA: *Buddha and the Gospel of Buddhism*. Harrap, 1916. *Hinduism and Buddhism*. Philosophical Library, New York.

The Dhammapada. Edited by J. Austin.

DUMOULIN-SASAKI: *The Development of Chinese Zen*. 1st Zen Institute of America, 1953.

EATON, GAI: *The Richest Vein*. Faber, 1949.

EVANS-WENTZ, W. Y.: *Tibetan Yoga and Secret Doctrines*. Oxford, 1935.

GABB, W.: *The Goose is Out*. The Buddhist Society, 1956.

HARE, LOFTUS: *Mysticism of East and West*. Cape, 1923.

HOWE, E. GRAHAM: *Mysterious Marriage*. Faber, 1949.

HUMPHREYS, CHRISTMAS: *Buddhism*. Penguin Books, 1951. *Concentration and Meditation*. The Buddhist Lodge (later Buddh. Society), 1935. *Karma and Rebirth*. John Murray, 1943. *Walk On!* The Buddhist Society, 1956. *Zen Buddhism*. Allen & Unwin, 1957.

HUXLEY, ALDOUS: *Adonis and the Alphabet*. Chatto & Windus, 1956. *The Perennial Philosophy*. Chatto & Windus, 1946.

JACOBI, J.: *The Psychology of C. G. Jung*. Kegan Paul, 1942.

JAMES, WILLIAM: *Varieties of Religious Experience*. Longmans, 1919.

JUDGE, W. Q. (Trans.): *Patanjali's Yoga Aphorisms*.

JUNG, C. G.: *Essays on Contemporary Events*. Kegan Paul, 1947. *Psychology and Religion*. Yale, 1938. *Psychological Types*. Kegan Paul, 1933. *The Integration of the Personality*. Kegan Paul, 1940. *The Undiscovered Self*. Routledge & Kegan Paul, 1958. *The Secret of the Golden Flower*. (See under R. Wilhelm).

Mahatma Letters to A. P. Sinnett, The. Second Edition. Ed. A. T. Barker. Rider, 1930.

MUNDY, TALBOT: *Om*. Hutchinson, 1925.

MURTI, T. R. V.: *The Central Philosophy of Buddhism*. Allen & Unwin, 1955.

MYERS, L. H.: *The Root and the Flower*. Cape, 1935.

NUKARIYA, KAITEN: *The Religion of the Samurai*. Luzac, 1913.

ROSS, FLOYD H.: *The Meaning of Life in Hinduism and Buddhism*. Routledge & Kegan Paul, 1952.

SANGHARAKSHITA, The Bhikshu: *A Survey of Buddhism*. The Indian Institute of World Culture, Bangalore, 1957.

SPIEGELBERG, F.: *Living Religions of the World*. Thames and Hudson, 1958.

SRI KRISHNA PREM: *The Yoga of the Kathopanishad*. Ananda Publishing House, Allahabad.

Sutra of Wei Lang (Hui-neng). Trans. Wong Mou-Lam for Buddhist Society. Luzac, 1944.

SUZUKI, D. T.: *Living by Zen*. Rider, 1950. *Zen Buddhism and its Influence on Japanese Culture*. The Eastern Buddhist Society, Kyoto, 1938. *Mysticism, Christian and Buddhist*. Allen & Unwin, 1957. *Essays in Zen Buddhism*, I (1927), II (1933), III (1934); all Luzac & Co. *The Essence of Buddhism*. The Buddhist Society, 1957. *An Introduction to Zen Buddhism*. Rider, 1948. *Studies in the Lankavatara Sutra*. Routledge, 1930.

Tao Tê Ching. Trans. Ch'u Ta-Kao. The Buddhist Society, 1937 (reprinting, Allen & Unwin, 1959).

TAKAKUSU, J.: *The Essentials of Buddhist Philosophy*. University of Hawai, 1947.

WATTS, ALAN W.: *The Wisdom of Insecurity*. Pantheon, New York, 1951. *The Way of Zen*. Thames and Hudson, 1957. *Nature, Man and Woman*. Thames and Hudson, 1958.

'WEI-WU-WEI': *Fingers Pointing Towards the Moon*. Routledge and Kegan Paul, 1958.

WILHELM, RICHARD. Trans.: *The Secret of the Golden Flower*. Kegan Paul, 1931

WOODS, CHARLOTTE: *The Self and its Problems*. Theosophical Publishing House, 1922.

A SELECTION OF RECENT BOOKS ON ZEN BUDDHISM

A FIRST ZEN READER, Trevor Leggett, Tuttle, 1960

THE BLUE CLIFF RECORDS, R. D. M. Shaw, Michael Joseph, 1961

THE ZEN TEACHING OF HUI HAI, trans. Blofeld, Rider, 1962

ZEN, A WAY OF LIFE, Christmas Humphreys, English Universities Press, 1962

THE EMBOSSED TEA KETTLE, Hakuin Zenji, George Allen & Unwin, 1963

THE TIGER'S CAVE, Trevor Leggett, Rider, 1964

THE MATTER OF ZEN, Wienpahl, New York University Press, 1964

THE FIELD OF ZEN, D. T. Suzuki, The Buddhist Society, 1964

THE ZEN KOAN, Miura and Ruth Sasaki, The First Zen Institute of America in Japan, 1965

ZEN AND ZEN CLASSICS, Vol. IV, *Mumonkan*, R. H. Blyth, Hokuseido Press, 1966

THREE PILLARS OF ZEN, Kapleau, Harper & Row, 1966

MYSTICS AND ZEN MASTERS, Thomas Merton, New Directions, 1967

ZEN AND THE BIRDS OF APPETITE, Thomas Merton, New Directions, 1968

ZEN MIND, BEGINNER'S MIND, SHUNRYU SUZUKI, Walker/Weatherhill, 1970

WHAT IS ZEN? D. T. Suzuki, Buddhist Society, 1971

A GLIMPSE OF NOTHINGNESS, Van de Wetering, Routledge & Kegan Paul, 1974

THE WISDOM OF ZEN MASTERS, Irmgard Schloegl, Sheldon, 1975

THE RECORD OF RINZAI, trans. Irmgard Schloegl, Buddhist Society, 1975

I CHING
The Chinese Book of Change

Translated by John Blofeld

Probably the oldest book in the world *The Book of Change* or *I-Ching* has been used for predicting the future for over 3,000 years. It is the most powerful distillation of Chinese wisdom, a remarkable combination of mathematical ingenuity and psychological intuition. It can be uncannily prophetic and is unfailingly intriguing.

Lama Anagarika Govinda, who has written a foreword to the book, has described it as 'one of the most profound books ever written'. Confucius said that if he had fifty years to live he would devote them to a study of *I-Ching*.

THE LIFE OF THE BUDDHA

H. Saddhatissa

The Venerable Dr H. Saddhatissa is a Buddhist monk and scholar with a deep knowledge of the Pali canon. He has written a beautiful and compellingly readable account of the Life of Guatama, the Buddha, from which the strength and gentleness of the Buddha's character emerge.

The day to day incidents of the Buddha's life and the allegories and parables in which he enveloped much of his teaching are presented with vividness and clarity.

LIGHT ON YOGA

B. K. S. Iyengar

Light on Yoga has long been recognised as the fullest, most practical and best illustrated book on yoga. This edition has its 600 illustrations newly positioned throughout the text to complement the 200 postures and 14 different exercises.

B. K. S. Iyengar has taught yoga for nearly 40 years. *Light on Yoga* provides a fully progressive course lasting over 300 weeks with advice about exercises for specific ailments.

MAN AND NATURE

The Spiritual Crisis of Modern Man

Seyyed Hossein Nasr

Seyyed Hossein Nasr explores ideas about Man and Nature in Taoism, Hinduism, Buddhism, Christianity and Islam, particularly its Sufi dimension. With deep insight and sensitivity he analyses the spiritual crisis of the twentieth century and stresses the importance of a greater awareness of the origins of Nature and Man.

'His knowledge of western scientific writing is profound ... his criticisms well documented.'

The Times Literary Supplement

UNDERSTANDING ISLAM

Frithjof Schuon

This book is regarded as a classic of its kind. Frithjof Schuon (described by T. S. Eliot as 'the most impressive writer in the field of comparative religion') explains the basis of Islamic belief 'from within'. Taking the theme that Islam is 'the meeting between God and Man', Schuon expounds the Islamic view of life, the role of the Prophet and the Quran, and the nature of Sufism and path of spiritual ascent.

'The best introduction to Islam as a religion and way of life.'
Seyyed Hossein Nasr, *Islamic Studies*

YOGA AND HEALTH

Selvarajan Yesudian and Elisabeth Haich

Yoga and Health has long been an international best-selling book on Yoga. Clear, readable and easy to use it demonstrates ways of developing and controlling muscles and breathing to enjoy a new and healthier way of life.

Translated into eighteen languages, *Yoga and Health* has already sold over one and a half million copies.

ZEN BUDDHISM

Christmas Humphreys

Zen has no God, nor dogma of any kind. It is not so much a religion as a way of perceiving, thinking, acting and being. With its unique methods of meditation, questioning, intuition and artistic cultivation, Zen can bring an amazing degree of spiritual, emotional and mental poise, together with an increased awareness of self, nature and the world.

'He presents a very comprehensive idea of Zen in all its aspects.'
World Buddhism

HARA

The Vital Centre of Man

Karlfried von Dürckheim

Have you ever wanted to change your life-style, to acquire a more relevant set of values, a more dynamic way of thinking, acting and existing?

'Hara' is Japanese for 'vital centre' – the vital centre of the self, the focus of existence. Its teaching is simple: see the whole self as a single entity, a union of body and soul, and you can attain a higher state of harmony and fulfilment. Instead of neurosis and stress, there will be inner calm and balance.

MANTRAS

Sacred Words of Power

John Blofeld

Mantras, the sacred formulae memorised for meditation in India, China and Tibet have attracted a great deal of attention. How do they work?

In this beautifully illustrated book John Blofeld explains the significance and operation of mantras. The efficacy of mantras as an aid to meditation is beyond doubt, but controversy surrounds the reasons for their success. John Blofeld approaches the subject with insight and sensitivity and with the benefit of first-hand encounters with monks and lamas.

RAMANA MAHARSHI

The Sage of Arunacala

T. M. P. Mahadevan

Rama Maharshi was one of the most saintly of Hindu ascetics and mystics, as well as one of the most intriguing. To his cave flocked many pilgrims, among them Jung and Somerset Maugham.

His philosophy is outstanding for its purity and gentleness. He preached that God, the self and the world are indivisible. Like St Francis of Assissi, he loved animals and advocated a life of tranquillity, non-violence and meditation.

Dr Mahadevan, the author of many books on Hindu thought, brings the teaching of Ramana Maharshi vividly to life.

SAMADHI

The Superconsciousness of the Future

Mouni Sadhu

Samadhi means 'superconsciousness'. Mouni Sadhu, the well-known author of *The Tarot, Concentration* and *Meditation* shows how to develop a keener state of awareness, achieve self-realization and attain a lasting sense of spirituality and inner peace.

TAO TÊ CHING

Translated by Ch'u Ta-Kao

Tao Tê Ching is the acknowledged masterpiece of Taoist philosophy. Written in beguilingly simple but enigmatic language, it has fascinated readers for over 2,000 years.

Tao Tê Ching embraces universal wisdom within a tiny compass and contains much insight for those who can unravel its message. This translation, the first by a modern Chinese scholar, powerfully conveys the beauty and vigour of the original.

YOGA FOR HEALTH AND VITALITY

M. J. Kirschner

Translated and edited by Lilian K. Donat

Yoga exercises not only for the young and athletic but also those who are unfit and overweight or suffering from the minor or major ailments that go with modern, urban life: muscular disorders, tension, heart trouble, depression and poor breathing are included in this book.

One of Europe's leading remedial yoga experts shows how as little as twenty minutes a day of yoga exercises will improve health and happiness.